Toward an East Asian Exchange Rate Regime

Toward an East Asian Exchange Rate Regime

DUCK-KOO CHUNG
BARRY EICHENGREEN
editors

BROOKINGS INSTITUTION PRESS
Washington, D.C.

ABOUT BROOKINGS

1775 Massachusetts Avenue, N.W., Washington, D.C. 20036
www.brookings.edu

Library of Congress Cataloging-in-Publication data
Toward an East Asian exchange rate regime / Duck-Koo Chung and Barry Eichengreen, editors.
p. cm.
Summary: "Analyzes the feasibility of continued exchange rate pegging in East Asia and explores alternatives, including some form of regional monetary integration. Argues for coordinating the adjustment of Asian currencies against the dollar and sketches scenarios for the creation of an Asian central bank and a single Asian currency"—Provided by publisher.
Includes bibliographical references and index.
ISBN-13: 978-0-8157-1419-4 (pbk. : alk. paper)
ISBN-10: 0-8157-1419-X (pbk. : alk. paper)
1. Foreign exchange rates—East Asia. 2. Monetary unions—East Asia. I. Chung, Duck-Koo, 1948– II. Eichengreen, Barry J. III. Title.
HG3976.5.T68 2007
332.4'56095—dc22 2006038536

1 3 5 7 9 8 6 4 2

Typeset in Adobe Garamond

Composition by R. Lynn Rivenbark
Macon, Georgia

Contents

Preface

EAST ASIAN MONETARY integration is an issue that will not go away. The desirability of an integrated regional response was first raised by its absence in the Asian financial crisis of 1997–98. The issue was highlighted further by adoption of the euro in 1999, which promised to free Europe from such problems once and for all. It was reinforced by the rapid de facto economic integration of the East Asian economies as a result of China's emergence as the assembly platform for the region's exports to the rest of the world and the consequent growth of intraregional trade and investment. Most recently the problem of global imbalances—shorthand for the large current account deficits of the United States and the massive accumulation of foreign assets, mainly dollar assets, by the Asian economies—has raised new questions about the sustainability of the current constellation of exchange rates. It has created pressure, both economic and political, for the realignment of Asian currencies against the dollar and encouraged arguments for a coordinated East Asian response.

But different observers continue to see the issue of what regional monetary arrangement is best for East Asia in different ways. Different diagnoses of the problem continue to complicate efforts to agree on a cooperative solution. So do the heterogeneity of economies within East Asia, the still unresolved legacies of military conflict and occupation in the first half of the twentieth century, and growing economic and financial rivalry between China and the United States.

These are among the observations prompting our effort to bring together leading economists from China, Japan, South Korea, and the United States to offer their diagnoses of the problem and assess the prospects for a concerted Asian response—in particular, one that might involve a higher level of regional cooperation, coordination, and integration. Despite the existence of continuing differences, which will become apparent below, we think that their discussions and analyses constitute a modest if still significant step toward the development of an intellectual and policy consensus.

First drafts of the papers collected in this volume were presented to a conference on the prospects for monetary integration in East Asia held in August 2005 in Seoul under the auspices of the Forum on East Asian Monetary Cooperation and with the support of the Ministry of Finance and Economy of the Government of Korea. We are grateful to Yunjong Wang and Gongpil Choi for their help in formulating the agenda and helping us move smoothly from conference papers to book manuscript. We thank Kookmin Bank, Shinhan Bank, Hana Bank, Samsung Insurance, SK Telecom, and GS Construction for lending financial support to the project. We are grateful to the staff at Brookings and to our editor, Nancy Morrison, for helping us move from manuscript into print.

It is said that a journey of a thousand miles must begin with the first step. In this spirit, we hope that the thoughts contained in this volume will provide at least modest impetus for the countries of East Asia to embark on the long and winding path leading ultimately to deeper regional monetary cooperation and integration.

DUCK-KOO CHUNG
National Assembly of Korea

BARRY EICHENGREEN
University of California–Berkeley

Toward an East Asian Exchange Rate Regime

1

DUCK-KOO CHUNG
BARRY EICHENGREEN

Exchange Rate Arrangements for Emerging East Asia

WHAT TO DO about exchange rate arrangements is high on the policy agenda of emerging East Asia.[1] For decades, export-led growth has been integral to national development strategies in countries like South Korea and Taiwan. More recently, other countries, China and Vietnam among them, have adopted this same approach to initiating and sustaining economic growth. An exchange rate that is stable and competitively valued has been seen as necessary for penetrating foreign markets and successfully implementing this strategy.[2] This is the lesson drawn from Japan's high growth era, when the yen was pegged to the dollar for more than two decades and the country succeeded in transforming itself into an industrial powerhouse on the basis of manufactured exports.[3] For more than a half century, economic growth has been the common objective around which East Asian governments and societies have coalesced,

1. Emerging East Asia is taken here as including the ten members of the Association of Southeast Asian Nations, or ASEAN (Brunei, Cambodia, Indonesia, Laos, Malaysia, Myanmar, the Philippines, Singapore, Thailand, and Vietnam), together with China, Hong Kong, South Korea, and Taiwan. The main difference between "emerging East Asia" and "East Asia" is Japan, which nonetheless figures prominently in the discussion below. Throughout this volume, "Korea" refers to South Korea.

2. See Sachs and Warner (1995) for a powerful statement of the conventional wisdom.

3. Two contrasting interpretations of this experience are McKinnon (2005) and Eichengreen and Hatase (2005). A reasonably stable and appropriately valued exchange rate is also a precondition for the other pillar of the East Asian growth model—attracting foreign direct investment (FDI), particularly into the export-processing sector.

and the export-based strategy has delivered the goods. Given the historical association of economic growth and exchange rate stability, it is not surprising that Asian policymakers continue to long for stable currencies.

This was the context that rendered the Asian financial crisis of 1997–98 so traumatic. The crisis wreaked havoc with prevailing currency values. It interrupted the rapid economic growth that countries had come to take for granted. It reminded governments and their constituents that if confidence in policies were disturbed, the country might find itself helpless in the face of the pressures emanating from global financial markets. It taught officials that national economies could feel negative effects from financial disturbances and sharp exchange rate movements elsewhere in the region. East Asia's unhappy experience with aid and conditionality from the International Monetary Fund (IMF) then provided a stark reminder that the region could not count on reliable help from outside.

For all these reasons, the restoration of prosperity, stability, and growth has come to be regarded synonymously with the restoration of order to the region's foreign exchange markets. This is not to say that everyone necessarily agrees on what "the restoration of order" entails or on what constitutes the best means to this end. And post-crisis reform entails more than merely exchange market reform: it involves improving prudential supervision, building deeper and more liquid financial markets, strengthening corporate governance, and cultivating the skills needed to build a knowledge-based, innovation-intensive economy. Still, discussions of this reform agenda rarely get far before commentators launch into discourses on the exchange rate problem.

Now, with the explosive growth of America's current account deficit and the emergence of global imbalances as the dominant problem on the international economic and financial scene, it is not only Asian policymakers who are preoccupied by this set of issues. East Asian exchange rates have become a flashpoint globally. U.S. officials argue that Asian exchange rates pegged to the dollar at artificially low levels are contributing to imbalances jeopardizing global economic stability, or at least that they are preventing their orderly resolution. Restoring balance to the interregional balance of payments and hence to the world economy requires of Asia a combination of expenditure switching and expenditure increasing policies: expenditure switching to shift production away from exports, and expenditure increasing to provide adequate demand for that production at home. The expenditure increasing can be brought about through additional public spending and by financial market development to encourage consumer borrowing and obviate the need for very high levels of household saving. The expenditure switching requires a change in relative prices that can be brought about either through higher inflation in Asia or appreciation of the region's currencies against the dollar. The latter is unambiguously preferable from the point of view of price stability and central bank credibility.

U.S. officials therefore argue for a substantial one-time revaluation of the Chinese renminbi in the hope that other East Asian countries will then permit their currencies to follow. Or they argue that China should move to an exchange rate regime entailing greater flexibility, under which the value of the currency is "market determined," permitting it to also adopt a more flexible monetary policy. Or they argue that East Asian central banks should agree on a joint float and collective appreciation of their currencies against the dollar.

For Asian policymakers, these issues constitute a dilemma. Officials recognize that resolving the problem of global imbalances requires the dollar to fall against other currencies, including their own. But greater exchange rate flexibility and appreciation against the currency of the country that is a key export market may not be compatible with their traditional reliance on export-led growth. In addition, the appreciation of local currencies against the dollar raises the specter of capital losses on the region's dollar reserves.

Some of these problems could conceivably be ameliorated by collective action. Thus capital losses on dollar reserves might be limited if the process of reserve diversification were cooperatively managed.[4] Rather than selling off dollar reserves in a rush, Asian central banks could cautiously inject them into the markets at times of relative dollar strength. Exchange rate volatility might be reduced if the adjustment of exchange rates against the dollar were coordinated within the region. This is the basis for the argument that East Asian countries should coordinate their response to the problem of global imbalances. Some proponents go a step further and argue that cooperative management of exchange rates and reserves would be facilitated by creating a common set of agreed currency targets and commitments: in other words, by agreeing on a regional exchange rate regime.

Probing Deeper

A coordinated response is most likely if the potential participants in such an initiative share a common diagnosis of the problem they are being asked to solve and of the effects of alternative solutions.[5] However, as soon as one starts probing deeper, one discovers that there is little agreement on the nature of the

4. A suggestion along these lines, for an international reserve standard, is made by Truman and Wong (2006).

5. This point has been made in different ways by Frankel and Rockett (1988) and Eichengreen and Uzan (1993).

problem, much less on what constitutes a solution. For some, the problem is how to engineer a joint appreciation against the dollar as a partial resolution of global imbalances, followed by measures to restore the stability of the dollar rate, reflecting the continuing importance of the United States as an export market and source of foreign direct investment (FDI). For others, the problem is how to enhance exchange rate stability within the region, given the rapid development of intra-Asian supply chains and vertical intra-industry trade. For still others, the problem is how to obtain greater exchange rate flexibility as a way of enhancing monetary autonomy and strengthening the incentive for banks and firms to hedge currency risks. Not all these diagnoses of the problem point with equal force to exchange rate stability as the focus of policy-coordination efforts.

Even if one accepts the premise that East Asia would benefit from stable exchange rates, this leaves open the question of "stable against what?" Even if one agrees that Asian countries should cooperate in engineering the joint appreciation of their currencies to help resolve the problem of global imbalances, this leaves open whether that joint appreciation should be against the dollar; the dollar and the euro; or even the dollar, the euro, and the yen: pointing in turn to the question of whether Japan should be inside or outside such an agreement. Similarly, even if one is committed to the idea that Asia's future lies in intraregional trade and investment, the question is whether other currencies should be pegged to the yen, Japan being the leading source of FDI in the region, or the renminbi, with China emerging as its leading supplier of exports and leading importer of components and raw materials.

Once upon a time the existence of the Bretton Woods system finessed this dilemma. In the 1950s and 1960s, when all currencies of consequence were pegged to the U.S. dollar, stabilizing a currency against the dollar automatically stabilized it against other currencies.[6] But with the collapse of the Bretton Woods system in the 1970s, the yen and the dollar began fluctuating against one another, so that stabilizing exchange rates against the dollar, the traditional East Asian strategy, was no longer equivalent to stabilizing them globally. Eventually the consequences came to be important. Thus the appreciation of the dollar against the yen in the mid-1990s, in conjunction with the maintenance of de jure or de facto dollar pegs by Asian central banks, was widely cited, with benefit of hindsight, as having undermined the export competitiveness of the East Asian economies and thereby contributed to the 1997–98 crisis.[7]

6. For details, see chapter 4 by Shin and Wang later in this volume.

7. Kwan (2001) has generalized this analysis of how fluctuations in the yen-dollar rate, in conjunction with central banks' de facto dollar pegging policies, have affected competitiveness and growth in the Asian economies.

Now it is anticipated that the Chinese renminbi will eventually be allowed to display more flexibility against the dollar.[8] In turn this will have wider implications for the efficacy of dollar pegging. As noted, China has already emerged as the most important trading partner and destination for the FDI of its East Asian neighbors. Assuming that the rapid growth of the Chinese economy is sustained, it will not be too many years before this is the case throughout East Asia. East Asia is effectively committed to a pattern of vertically integrated intra-industry trade in which China—and, increasingly, other low-wage East Asian economies—import capital goods, parts, and components so as to act as assembly platforms for the region's exports of final goods to the rest of the world. Here, again, volatility of exchange rates among the participating countries could disrupt established economic relations. For those impressed by China's rise but who also value exchange rate stability, the question is increasingly: stability against the dollar or stability against the renminbi?

We should not leave the impression that the case for exchange rate stability is universally accepted. Some argue that the problem leading up to the Asian crisis was not that central banks and governments were inadequately committed to stabilizing their exchange rates but, to the contrary, that they were too slow to recognize the need for greater flexibility.[9] With the development of their economies and financial markets—and with accession to the Organization for Economic Cooperation and Development (OECD), in the case of South Korea—exposure to capital flows was heightened.[10] So long as exchange rates were pegged, growing capital mobility left less scope for autonomous monetary policies that might prevent economies from overheating and protect them from potentially dangerous lending booms. Monetary conditions were increasingly linked to those in the United States—such is the unavoidable implication of the combination of a pegged dollar exchange rate and high capital mobility—and monetary conditions in the United States were not obviously appropriate to conditions in Asia, where economies were at different stages of development and experienced fluctuations, for both economic and political reasons, on a different cycle. In practice, monetary policy became increasingly procyclical; since nominal interest rates were increasingly equalized across countries, faster growing

8. In July of 2005 the Chinese authorities took a first step in this direction, revaluing the renminbi by 2.1 percent against the dollar, and announcing that henceforth the exchange rate would be managed with reference to a basket of currencies and allowed to exhibit greater flexibility. In practice, however, the renminbi-dollar rate was allowed to exhibit little additional flexibility in the course of the immediately succeeding months. This Chinese policy initiative is discussed further in a number of the chapters that follow.

9. This is the conclusion of Goldstein (1998), for example.

10. The obligations of OECD membership required South Korea to relax and remove its capital controls following its accession to that body in 1996.

economies with higher inflation rates experienced lower real interest rates at the worst possible time. Meanwhile, one-time changes in the exchange rate against the dollar became more difficult to engineer as the capital account of the balance of payments opened. And so long as the exchange rate ostensibly remained pegged, banks and corporations had little incentive to hedge their foreign currency exposures—since the authorities continued to reassure them, all the while, that the price of foreign currency would not be changed.

The solution to these problems, according to some economists, is not to restore exchange rate stability but instead to move to greater flexibility, using a band-based system à la Singapore or an inflation targeting regime like that adopted by Korea in recent years.[11] East Asian countries need more monetary autonomy and room for maneuver, not just vis-à-vis the United States but relative to one another, since they are a heterogeneous lot. Since levels of economic and financial development differ among them, different exchange rates and, more fundamentally, different exchange rate regimes are desirable in different national cases. In this view, simply replacing dollar pegs with yen pegs, yen-euro-dollar basket pegs, or an intraregional currency grid would be a retrograde step.

Not for the first time, different economists are able to discern support for these different positions in the same set of data. East Asian currency regimes, it would appear, are a bit like a Rorschach test: there is a tendency for economists to see in their evolution more or less what they expect. Ronald McKinnon, a believer in the merits of pegging to the dollar, observes the relatively limited volatility of currencies against the greenback and concludes that this is evidence of the resurrection of the de facto East Asian dollar standard.[12] Leonardo Hernandez and Peter Montiel, who are more convinced of the merits of flexibility, look at the same data and conclude that the majority of East Asian countries have moved to at least somewhat greater flexibility.[13] The safest conclusion is probably that East Asian countries have not all moved in the same direction. As Masahiro Kawai shows in chapter 5 later in this volume, there is a growing diversity of arrangements. Thus while Hong Kong maintains its dollar-based currency peg and Taiwan continues to stabilize its exchange rate against the dollar even more tightly than before the crisis, Indonesia, the Philippines, Singapore, South Korea, and Thailand have all moved to at least somewhat greater flexibility against the dollar. China and Malaysia appear to be in transition between these two states.

11. See Goldstein (2002).
12. See McKinnon (2005).
13. See Hernandez and Montiel (2003).

Debate over what exchange rate regime is best in general has been ongoing for the better part of the last century. Many economists probably subscribe to Jeffrey Frankel's (1999) conclusion that no single regime is best at all times and places—that the only general answer to the question of which regime is best is "it depends." If so, it would also seem to follow that no single regime is right for all of East Asia. The region is made up of very heterogeneous economies, ranging from the high-income Japan to the low-income Myanmar, from the technologically sophisticated South Korea and Taiwan to the much less technologically advanced Cambodia and Vietnam, from the heavily agricultural Laos to the entirely urban and industrial Singapore. It is hard to imagine that a single set of monetary and financial arrangements could be suitable for all members of this eclectic grouping. In a sense the growing diversity of exchange rate arrangements in the region is itself evidence of this fact.

To be sure, western Europe is a diverse subcontinent as well, and that diversity has not prevented it from successfully navigating the transition to a common regime—indeed to the most uniform such regime, a common currency. But, by most measures, levels of diversity are even greater in East Asia.

Precedents and Proposals

Proposals for currency reform, perhaps predictably, are equally diverse. These range from recommendations that Asian countries should all move to floating exchange rates, backed by some form of open-economy inflation targeting, to plans for a swift transition to a single regional currency. Other alternatives lie between these ends of the spectrum. These include the idea that the emerging markets of East Asia should adopt basket pegs against the dollar, euro, and yen, which will better insulate them from disturbances associated with changes in the yen-dollar and yen-euro rates while still encouraging trade and financial flows with the rest of the world. They include the idea that by adopting the same basket weights and pegging relatively strictly to that basket, emerging East Asian economies might at the same time succeed in stabilizing their exchange rates against one another. The obvious objection here is that while substituting a G-3 currency basket for the dollar as the reference point for policy reduces exposure to yen-dollar and yen-euro fluctuations, it eliminates none of the other problems associated with external anchors that came home to roost in the Asian crisis and that will arise again if East Asian countries adopt such a basket and again peg to it relatively strictly.[14]

14. Many of these same points are powerfully made by Reinhart and Reinhart (2003).

Alternatively, it is argued that emerging East Asia should concentrate on stabilizing intraregional exchange rates rather than exchange rates vis-à-vis the United States, Europe, and Japan. Intraregional trade has been the most rapidly growing component of East Asia's total trade. Regional supply chains and production networks are best fostered by limiting exchange rate variability within the region, not by limiting variability vis-à-vis the rest of the world. Since exchange rate stability is valued by foreign investors, stable intra-Asian exchange rates may be important for encouraging the cross-border participation in local currency bond markets that is the goal of the Asian Bond Fund and the Asian Bond Market Initiative.[15] These observations provide the motivation for proposals that East Asian countries agree on the creation and maintenance of a multilateral regional currency grid analogous to the European Snake of the 1970s and the European Monetary System (EMS) of the 1980s and 1990s, which stabilized exchange rates among the participating European countries, to one degree or another, while allowing them to float against the dollar and the yen—and not incidentally paved the way for the creation of a single regional currency.

An objection to this line of reasoning is that Europe's experience with the EMS and now with the euro has not been entirely happy. The stability of the EMS rested on the presence of capital controls; as soon as these were removed, in the early 1990s, the incompatibility of an intraregional currency grid, open capital markets, and political pressures for central banks to temper their exchange rate commitments manifested itself in a dramatic way, namely in the currency crises of 1992–93. Only after bands were widened and a deadline was set for the transition to monetary union—and countries like the United Kingdom and Sweden reluctant to move in that direction were permitted to drop out and adopt more flexible exchange rates—did that instability recede. This reading of European experience suggests that Asian countries would expose themselves to the same risk of instability if they prematurely adopted a regional currency grid: more so to the extent that international capital mobility has risen further in the intervening decade.

Nor would all observers necessarily give high marks to Europe's experience with its single currency. Monetary cohabitation has not been an entirely happy experience for the participating countries. Some fast-growing European countries would have benefited from a tighter monetary policy. Such a policy, for example, would have helped Ireland by limiting the excesses associated with its housing boom. Meanwhile, other slower-growing countries, such as Germany, would have preferred a looser policy. But both preferences could not be accom-

15. For more on these initiatives, see chapter 3 by Yu and chapter 5 by Kawai later in this volume.

modated, given a single currency and a single monetary policy. More recently, there has been the emergence of serious problems of international competitiveness in countries like Italy, which have been disproportionately hit by the growth of Chinese competition given their industrial structures. In the presence of a national currency, adjustment can be facilitated by a discrete devaluation, which steps down domestic currency labor costs, assuming limited compensatory wage inflation. In the absence of such a currency, adjustment can take place only through a grinding deflation, which draws out the pain. This suggests that East Asia might similarly experience severe discomfort if it attempted to fit all the countries of the region into a single monetary straitjacket.

To be sure, this may be an overly pessimistic reading of Europe's experience with the euro. Monetary union has succeeded in eliminating exchange rate instability among the participating countries. It has ring-fenced Europe against financial instability emanating from outside, precisely as its architects intended. Indeed, it is hard to imagine that there would have been no exchange rate problems among the members of the euro area in the face of the September 11, 2001, terrorist attacks in the United States, the Madrid bombings, or the Iraq war, had a dozen regional currencies still been in circulation. This success at ring-fencing the region against outside financial pressures will have considerable appeal to Asian observers, especially in light of the interpretation of the 1997–98 crisis that implicates instability in global financial markets.[16]

Another objection to the presumption that East Asia should follow the European example is that other regions, notably North America, have been able to make significant progress in regional economic integration without stabilizing their exchange rates, much less moving toward a regional currency arrangement. The North American Free Trade Agreement (NAFTA) has led to the very significant further elaboration of supply chains and production linkages between the three participating economies since its establishment in the first half of the 1990s. The production of motor vehicles and parts, to take one example, is increasingly linked across North America's internal borders.[17] The northern part of Mexico is increasingly specialized in assembly and production operations for the U.S. market. That the Canadian dollar and Mexican peso continue to fluctuate against the U.S. dollar has not obviously posed an obstacle to the progress of real economic integration.[18]

16. On this view, see for example chapter 3 by Yu.

17. See Arndt (2006).

18. Indeed, not just the Canadian dollar but also the Mexican peso have been allowed to fluctuate increasingly freely against the U.S. dollar over time, as the Bank of Mexico has moved to an inflation targeting regime and shunned intervention in the foreign exchange market.

One can argue that the compatibility of exchange rate variability with production integration in North America reflects the unusual availability of hedging instruments. Forward exchange rate contracts are freely available on both sides of the U.S.-Canadian border, while Mexican peso futures can be bought and sold on the Chicago Mercantile Exchange. Producers in Asia, for their part, lack such markets, making it harder for them to hedge the associated risks; hence exchange rate fluctuations will be more disruptive to trade. But the availability of hedging instruments is in part a function of demand. If Asian currencies are allowed to move more freely, the increased demand for hedges will help to stimulate the demand of the relevant forward and futures markets—although how quickly remains to be seen.[19]

One can also argue that exchange rates within North America have been unusually predictable because the region's three central banks have all been following stable monetary policies, the Bank of Canada and Bank of Mexico, in particular, in the context of inflation targeting regimes. The evidence suggests that credible inflation targeters have more stable exchange rates, other things equal, minimizing the volatility that is arguably disruptive to regional integration.[20] Asia has less experience with inflation targeting, creating worries that abandoning its traditional exchange rate–centered monetary policy strategy might open the door to volatility that would interfere with regional integration. The counterargument is that there is no fundamental obstacle to the successful pursuit of inflation targeting in the region.[21]

European and North American experience also differ in two further respects. First, the European model in which the integration of markets in goods and services is accompanied by a regional exchange rate stabilization arrangement leading ultimately to the creation of a single currency is more obviously conducive to financial market integration. The advent of the euro has had a strong positive impact on the growth of cross-border financial transactions and on the growth of a regional corporate bond market in particular.[22] This reduced funding costs for European corporations, which have used their new access to debt finance to undertake mergers and acquisitions, a process that should ultimately result in some further rationalization of European industry

19. This is a lesson of the same Japanese experience in the era of high growth referred to in the opening paragraph. There the absence of deep and liquid forward markets in foreign exchange was cited as an impediment to greater exchange rate flexibility. As things turned out the advent of greater exchange rate flexibility prompted the development of deeper and more liquid forward markets.

20. Eichengreen and Taylor (2004) provide econometric evidence to this effect.

21. For more discussion of this argument and its limitations, see chapter 6 by Choi later in this volume.

22. A good summary of bond market developments in Europe since 1999 is Pagano and von Thadden (2004).

and improvement in the region's international competitiveness. Officials also see the development of deep and liquid regional financial markets as a step toward making the euro a serious rival to the dollar as an international currency, something that has been an objective of European politicians since at least the time of Charles de Gaulle. If Asia's goal is not just economic integration, as in North America, but also financial integration, as in Europe, then the case for following the European model is correspondingly stronger.

Second, Europe's commitment to exchange rate stability was buttressed by its pursuit of other regional programs like the Common Agricultural Policy (CAP), whose operation was vulnerable to exchange rate fluctuations, especially in its early years.[23] Under the CAP, European governments sought to stabilize domestic currency prices for agricultural products in several countries simultaneously, something that would have been impossible in the face of persistent large-scale fluctuations in the exchange rates between them.[24] Asia may or may not be similarly inclined to establish sectoral price support programs; economists, at least, would generally hope not. But the case for exchange rate stabilization and hence for an EMS-like system is correspondingly stronger in the presence of such programs.

That there is a strong case for regional monetary integration tends to be taken for granted in Asia. An economic analysis suggests that here, as in many circumstances, there are trade-offs. Pursuing monetary integration entails giving up something else, namely monetary autonomy at the national level. Sacrificing the latter is not costless, as is evident in Europe's own experience since 1999. Whether doing so is desirable depends not just on an assessment of these costs but on one's view of what Asia is ultimately trying to achieve.

Politics

A further objection to the notion that Asia should attempt to put in place a regional mechanism resembling the European Monetary System is that the operation of such a system has formidable political preconditions, and that Asia differs from Europe to an even greater extent politically than economically.

23. This point was famously made by Giavazzi and Giovannini (1989).

24. If exchange rates had been allowed to move, there would have been strong incentives for cross-border arbitrage, undermining price floors in the countries whose currencies appreciated. Europe attempted to finesse this problem by creating a system of de facto dual exchange rates (the so-called "green rates" of the CAP alongside the market rates that applied to other transactions), but this only created inefficiencies and further incentives for arbitrage (between the two rates, where possible).

Stabilizing exchange rates within the region requires, first and foremost, harmonizing monetary policies and conditions. In Europe there existed a natural focal point for such efforts: namely, the monetary policies of the German Bundesbank, whose commitment to sound and stable policies was beyond reproach. Moreover, it was palatable to delegate responsibility for the common monetary policy to the Bundesbank because monetary cooperation was part of a larger political bargain. In effect, other European countries agreed to assign responsibility for the common monetary policy to Germany because Germany was prepared to defer to the others in the formulation of the common foreign and security policy. As this was sometimes put, the European Monetary System and then Economic and Monetary Union were devices for locking a peaceful Germany into Europe. Or, in a more narrowly economic formulation, the European Commission in Brussels delegated the common monetary policy to Germany in return for Germany's agreeing to participate in a broader process of economic integration led by Brussels.

East Asia lacks an analog to the Bundesbank. Japanese monetary policy in the first half of the 1990s was hardly a paragon of stability, and since then the Bank of Japan has followed a policy of quantitative easing (associated with near-zero interest rates) appropriate for the exceptional economic and financial circumstances of that country but unsuitable for the region as a whole. The People's Bank of China has been allowing that country's monetary and credit aggregates to expand at rates approaching 20 per cent per year, which makes sense for a country growing by 10 percent a year and experiencing a process of progressive monetization but which is again unsuitable for the larger region. East Asia's own paragon of stability, the Monetary Authority of Singapore, makes policy for a small, specialized economy whose ups and down are governed by the global high-tech industry, leading it to adopt policies that are less than ideal for its neighbors.

Even more fundamentally, Asia lacks a political setting that would make unilateral leadership by a single national central bank acceptable. China would be reluctant for reasons stemming from history to put its monetary fate in the hands of Japan, and vice versa. Korea would be understandably reluctant to assign its monetary policy to either of its larger neighbors.

These observations encourage talk of a multilateral currency arrangement in which each country defines its parity relative to the other participating currencies or to a weighted average of a group of regional currencies.[25] This symmetri-

25. This weighted average might be given a name in order to encourage its use as an accounting unit; it might be called the "Asian Currency Unit" (or ACU), in parallel with the European Currency Unit (or ECU) established in the 1970s.

cal arrangement would be more acceptable, the argument goes, because all participating countries would be on an equal footing. But this ignores the fact that virtually all multilateral systems in the past have operated as de facto follow-the-leader arrangements. In every historical case of note, one national currency has emerged as the "sun" around which the other national currencies revolve. This was true of the gold standard, when Britain acted as "conductor of the international orchestra," of the Bretton Woods system, when the U.S. dollar was the key currency, and of the EMS itself, which had been intended as a symmetrical multilateral regime but soon evolved into a German-led system.[26]

This outcome is not surprising. Creating a multilateral currency grid does not eliminate the need for a monetary anchor. Logically, the anchor will be the country with the soundest policies and the deepest financial markets. That country will have the prerogative of deciding the monetary policy to be followed by the entire grouping. It will therefore have disproportionate sway over the operation of the system.[27]

When contemplating such schemes, it is important to recall that individual Asian currencies are small boats adrift on highly liquid international financial markets. They can be buffeted by waves of speculation, and stabilizing them may require extensive foreign assistance. In the economist's lingo, extensive financial assistance may be needed for the credibility of the currency arrangement.[28] But countries will agree to support their neighbors financially only if they think that doing so will be productive and only if they are confident of being paid back. In turn this requires confidence that the recipients of their largesse will undertake the requisite policy adjustments. And this supposes firm surveillance of national policies. Asian countries would have to agree to firm regional oversight of their policies—and specifically to accepting blunt criticism when things go wrong or even threaten to go wrong. This is not the

26. A forceful statement of this view is Giovannini (1989).

27. Until, that is, the participating central banks are prepared to take the next, momentous step of creating a transnational central bank under their common control responsible for conducting the common monetary policy. This, of course, is the key step toward monetary union, which is a much more ambitious scheme for regional monetary reform than under discussion here. It is sometimes suggested that perhaps Japan and China would serve as the dual motors for East Asian monetary integration, analogous to the dual roles of France and Germany in European integration. This would of course require a level of diplomatic rapprochement and political comity that the two Asian powers have not yet begun to display. Moreover, there is the objection that while France and Germany worked together to push forward the larger European project, when it came to the Snake and the European Monetary System there was room for only one leader—the country with the strongest and most stable monetary policies—and that was Germany.

28. Otherwise, speculators may think that by engaging in extensive sales of a currency they may be able to ratchet up the pressure on the authorities sufficiently that the latter feel compelled to abandon the peg, as in so-called second generation models of balance of payments crises.

"Asian way," which is instead characterized by deference to one's neighbors' policies and a reluctance to engage in overt criticism.

This raises questions about whether the kind of extensive financial supports needed for the operation of a multilateral currency grid are feasible in East Asia. One sees the tension in the design of the Chiang Mai Initiative, the network of bilateral swap arrangements negotiated among ASEAN+3 countries starting in 2000.[29] Extension of these swaps beyond the first 15 percent is contingent on the negotiation of a program and hence subject to the conditionality of the International Monetary Fund.[30] In effect, qualms on the part of the funders about whether firm surveillance can be exercised led them to delegate this surveillance function to an outside authority. There continues to be talk of the desirability of "multilateralizing" the Chiang Mai Initiative, so that currency swap agreements, now negotiated between pairs of countries, come to be made available to the entire regional grouping. Whether the goal is desirable depends on one's view of the advisability of establishing and attempting to defend a regional currency grid. Whether it is practical hinges on the development of political solidarity sufficient to render individual Asian countries comfortable with delegating control over their financial resources to their partners in the regional arrangement.

Thus ensuring that countries pursue the requisite high levels of policy harmonization and guaranteeing them adequate levels of support in the face of market pressures will require a higher level of political solidarity than currently prevails in East Asia. A decade ago it was easy to dismiss schemes for an East Asian monetary union on political grounds.[31] The region lacked a tradition of integrationist thought comparable to that of postwar Europe. China and Japan, unlike France and Germany, did not draw from the experience of World War II the lesson that the way to prevent future conflicts was by pursuing a politically led integration process. However, now that Asian countries have had time to digest the lessons of the 1997–98 crisis, there are signs that this may be changing. Countries realize that the only way for the ascending region to exert power comparable to that projected by the United States and Europe is for its members to act collectively. They understand that regional problems like the underdevelopment of local financial markets will be easier to solve if they act collectively rather than individually. This new commitment to regional cooperation is evident in the Chiang Mai Initiative and the Asian Bond Fund. The readiness of East Asian governments and central banks to commit

29. On this, see chapter 3 by Yu.

30. Originally this was the first 10 percent, but the ratio was raised subsequently.

31. See for example Bayoumi, Eichengreen, and Mauro (2000).

meaningful financial resources to these regional initiatives signals a departure from the status quo ante.

These steps, however consequential, are also reminders of how far East Asia has to go before it will be in a position to create a durable system of regional currency pegs, much less a regional monetary union. Much more will have to be done in terms of cultivating political solidarity and cohesion. That completing this process took Europe half a century does not mean that it will necessarily take that long in Asia; the follower economies of Asia having shown the capacity to telescope into a shorter period processes that took longer in other parts of the world. But neither does it suggest that the process will be completed overnight.

In addition, the fact that political circumstances are different than in Europe suggests that the process of ongoing integration leading ultimately to monetary unification will be more market led and less politically led than was the case in Europe. European integration, it is sometimes said, was at root a political process; the Common Market and then EMU were economic means to a political end. In Asia, in contrast, markets play a larger role, and politicians a smaller one, in driving forward the integration process. This is clearly evident in trade integration, where the completion of the ASEAN Free Trade Area and now an ASEAN+3 Free Trade Area have been slow, but de facto integration propelled by vertical intra-industry trade and the associated FDI has been rapid. One way of thinking about the challenge facing East Asian policymakers—and one of the ways it is put in the remaining chapters of this book—is how to best enlist economic forces in furthering these processes.

The Chapters of This Book

These are the issues taken up in the chapters of this book. Chapter 2 by Masaru Yoshitomi of the Research Institute of Economy, Trade and Industry (RIETI) in Tokyo sets the stage by placing the Asian currency issue against the backdrop of the global imbalances problem. Yoshitomi warns that the U.S. external position is unsustainable and that the differential returns on U.S. foreign liabilities and assets that have prevented the country's foreign debt from exploding can no longer be counted on as in the past. He acknowledges the need for some collective appreciation of Asian currencies against the dollar to contribute to global rebalancing but worries that this adjustment could be stymied by the existence of a prisoner's dilemma. Even if countries recognize the need for their currencies to strengthen against the dollar as group, in other words, they may be reluctant to allow them to adjust individually if they are skeptical that their regional neighbors will do the same, both because they see that revaluation by any one country—even China—will not be enough to make a significant dent in the imbalances problem (for this, Asian countries will have to move together), and because they fear that if other countries do not respond in kind the initiating country will incur a double competitive disadvantage: not only will it lose competitiveness against the United States, but it will also lose competitiveness relative to its Asian neighbors.

Yoshitomi argues that the coordination of policies will be easiest if all countries in the region operate the same exchange rate regime. In particular, if all of them frame policy with reference to the same or at least a similar currency basket, and if they all maintain relatively wide fluctuation bands against it, then it will be relatively straightforward to negotiate and implement a regionally coordinated appreciation vis-à-vis the dollar. It would also be helpful, he concludes, to build stronger regional institutions to enhance the credibility of commitments to such a move.

In chapter 3, Yongding Yu of the Chinese Academy of Social Sciences asks who will lead the process of regional monetary and financial integration. He describes how interest in exchange rate cooperation was spurred by dissatisfaction with the IMF's response to the 1997–98 crisis and observes that these concerns have not gone away. He notes further than Japan's influence in Asia has tended to wane as a result of its extended economic slump. But he warns that China, the heir apparent to the throne, is preoccupied by its own reform agenda. Conceivably, leadership on monetary and financial issues could be provided jointly, but here lack of trust and rivalry between China and Japan is a problem.

Yu concludes that China as the rising power will unavoidably set the tone for discussions of East Asian monetary integration in coming years. But, in turn, this implies that the pace of progress will be slow. China has its own problems, and it will take time for it to complete the transition to a market economy. Once that has happened, China will be able to devote more attention and exert more leadership on regional matters. But at that point, domestic demand will have caught up with economic growth, and the country will have become less oriented toward exports and therefore less preoccupied by exchange rate issues, in much the same way that the United States is less preoccupied by them. Hence it is likely to become more skeptical about calls for a common basket peg or a regional exchange rate stabilization arrangement, much less a common currency. This suggests that a process of Asian monetary integration dependent on Chinese leadership or even contingent on significant Chinese participation is likely to be a slow one.

In chapter 4, Kwanho Shin of Korea University and Yunjong Wang of the SK Research Institute delve further into the connections between trade integration and monetary integration. That Europe first created a customs union before moving to monetary integration has fostered expectations that East Asia will do likewise. But efforts to complete the ASEAN Free Trade Area have been slow, and the obstacles to an ASEAN+3 free trade area are even more formidable. Given that there is a desire for exchange rate stabilization, this raises the question: why not capitalize on this predisposition by first stabilizing exchange rates, which will encourage the growth of intraregional trade and endogenously generate support for trade liberalization—support that will then feed back positively to the campaign for monetary integration?

For this strategy to be feasible there must be robust feedback from exchange rate stabilization to trade, and this requires that trade liberalization must have first reached a critical facilitating stage. Shin and Wang ask whether this is the case in Asia: whether there is evidence that limiting exchange rate volatility significantly stimulates trade and enhances the trade-creating effects of regional and bilateral free trade agreements. Their findings are mixed: while there is evidence of the direct positive effect of more stable exchange rates on trade, its magnitude is small by the standards of Europe. And, in contrast to Europe, the indirect effect magnifying the trade-creating effects of free trade areas appears to be missing. On balance, the authors are skeptical that monetary integration can lead trade integration in Asia, as opposed to following it as in Europe.

In chapter 5, Masahiro Kawai of the Asian Development Bank (ADB) and the University of Tokyo approaches the question of what reference point is best for East Asian currencies by exploring the past and future of international currency competition. He observes that the traditional situation where the dollar was unrivaled in the international monetary and financial sphere is unlikely to persist. The advent of the euro has already created serious competition for the dollar.[32] A relevant question in this context is whether one or more Asian currencies might also emerge as rivals. Kawai cautions that both the yen and the renminbi have drawbacks from this point of view. Japanese growth has been poor, and the zero yield on Japanese government bonds (JGBs) has made holding them as international reserves unattractive. China for its part has major

32. This is especially true if one accepts the argument, advanced by Lyons and Moore (2005) and Eichengreen (2005), that the network effects that once made international currency competition—reserve currency competition in particular—a winner-take-all game are unlikely to operate as powerfully in a twenty-first century world where the existence of sophisticated financial markets and instruments will minimize the costs of switching between currencies and using a variety of them in both domestic and international transactions.

structural problems; it is still far from a market economy. Until the transition to a market economy and an open political system is complete, agents will not be fully comfortable in using its currency for international transactions.

Even if no single Asian currency emerges as a serious rival to the dollar, a collection or basket of such currencies still could. Kawai suggests what East Asian governments and central banks can do to foster movement in this direction. Countries would first agree on a common G-3 basket peg, which would have the corollary benefits of limiting the volatility of intraregional rates and encouraging the use of local currencies in intraregional transactions. After strengthening surveillance, coordinating policies, and enlarging mutual supports, they could then create a truly multilateral Asian system along the lines of Europe's Snake and Exchange Rate Mechanism. Alternatively, they could increase the weight on the yen, in the limit transforming the G-3 basket into a yen bloc and stabilizing intra-Asian exchange rates still further. This approach would require dedicated Japanese leadership and a robust Japanese economy to make it more attractive for central banks and international investors to hold yen-denominated assets.

In chapter 6, Gongpil Choi of the Korean Institute of Finance and the Federal Reserve Bank of San Francisco also proposes a phased transition, although the details of his blueprint differ. While under the Choi plan the emerging economies of East Asia would again start by agreeing to formulate their monetary policies with reference to a common G-3 currency basket, they would be permitted to follow that common basket with different degrees of rigidity, in conformance with their different economic circumstances and conditions. Some regional currencies would fluctuate significantly against that basket, while others would follow it quite strictly. Consequently, in this first stage, intra-Asian exchange rates would continue to vary. Over time, strengthened surveillance and more extensive financial supports would permit governments and central banks to harmonize their policies more closely. As that harmonization proceeds, their policies toward the common external basket would be harmonized as well, and intraregional exchange rates would grow more stable. At this point the countries of the region would logically shift to a regional currency grid or local currency basket. From a multilateral currency grid or regional exchange rate stabilization agreement, the next logical step—which presumably would be a long way down the road—would be to a single East Asian currency and an East Asian Central Bank.

In contrast to these politically directed transition paths, in chapter 7 Barry Eichengreen of the University of California–Berkeley sketches a market-led approach. This would start with the creation of a synthetic regional unit—the

Asian Currency Unit, or ACU—that would be allowed to circulate in parallel with existing national currencies. This parallel currency would not replace national currencies, but it would circulate alongside them; in particular, it would have full legal tender status in the sponsoring countries. It would be more stable than existing national units in terms of aggregate East Asian trade and financial flows, and as such it should become increasingly attractive as a unit for keeping accounts, invoicing transactions, and making payments for governments, firms, and others engaged in significant cross-border transactions. Banks would presumably accept ACU deposits to meet these needs and match these with ACU loans; the stability of the parallel currency would also make it an attractive unit in which to issue regional bonds. All these uses of the parallel currency should become more extensive with the continuing growth of cross-border transactions within the region. Once the parallel currency gained popularity and acquired significant market share, it would it be clear that the time was ripe for the adoption of a single regional currency. Since residents would already be using this unit for the bulk of their transactions, eliminating national currencies in favor of the new unit would be painless at this point.

An important difference between this proposal and those of previous chapters is that it would not be necessary to limit the variability of East Asian exchange rates against one another. As Eichengreen notes, it would also be possible to establish a parallel currency defined as a basket of the currencies of the participating countries without adopting any peg at all. All that would be needed would be a set of rules and interventions that would maintain the ACU's value relative to the specified basket of regional currencies. If the constituent currencies floated against one another, then the ACU would rise in value relative to currencies that depreciated against the basket and fall in value relative to currencies that appreciated against the basket, without its value changing relative to the basket as a whole. Thus there is a distinction between the decision to establish a parallel currency defined as a basket of regional currencies and the decision to adopt a harmonized system of currency pegs—a point that all too often tends to be misunderstood.

This approach has the attraction that the pace of the transition to monetary union would be market led rather than politically led, consistent with the greater emphasis of Asian policymakers on market forces since the crisis of 1997–98. Its corresponding drawback—if it indeed is a drawback—is that the transition could be a lengthy one. Europe experimented with a parallel currency approach starting in the 1970s but ultimately gave it up for a more top-down politically driven strategy for creating a monetary union within a fixed period of time.

Summing Up

In sum, the authors contributing to this volume find common ground in the need for cooperation on exchange rate management in East Asia. They agree on the desirability of regional monetary integration. Despite coming from different places and adopting different perspectives, they concur on the need for greater flexibility of Asian currencies against the dollar in general and specifically to address the problem of global imbalances. At the same time, they acknowledge that the growth of intraregional trade—vertically oriented intra-industry trade, in particular—along with growing intraregional FDI flows creates a case for maintaining a reasonable degree of intra-Asian exchange rate stability. Together these observations create an argument that East Asian countries should coordinate the adjustment of their currencies against the dollar. Turning to the specifics of how they should do this, there is less of a consensus. Rather, there are a variety of plans.

For the longer run, the difficulty of holding stable the exchange rates of separate sovereign currencies suggests the desirability of deeper monetary integration, culminating in the creation of a regional central bank and a regional currency. But how this transition will occur, and under whose leadership, remains unclear. All this suggests that progress will be incremental and that the transition will not be complete anytime soon. Fortunately, Asian societies are not unfamiliar, or necessarily uncomfortable, with processes that take very long periods of time to unfold.

References

Arndt, Sven. 2006. "Regional Currency Arrangements in North America." Working Paper 121. Vienna: Austrian National Bank (May).

Bayoumi, Tamim, Barry Eichengreen, and Paulo Mauro. 2000. "On Regional Monetary Arrangements for ASEAN." *Journal of the Japanese and International Economies* 14 (June): 121–48.

Eichengreen, Barry. 2005. "Sterling's Past, Dollar's Future? Historical Perspectives on Reserve Currency Competition." Working Paper 11336. Cambridge, Mass.: National Bureau of Economic Research (May).

Eichengreen, Barry, and Mariko Hatase. 2005. "Can a Rapidly-Growing, Export-Oriented Economy Smoothly Exit an Exchange Rate Peg? Lessons for China from Japan's High Growth Era." Working Paper 11625. Cambridge, Mass.: National Bureau of Economic Research (September).

Eichengreen, Barry, and Alan Taylor. 2004. "The Monetary Consequences of a Free Trade Area of the Americas." In *Integrating the Americas: FTAA and Beyond,* edited by Antoni

Estevadeordal, Dani Rodrik, Alan Taylor, and Andrés Velasco, pp.189–226. David Rockefeller Center Series on Latin American Studies, Harvard University Press.

Eichengreen, Barry, and Marc Uzan. 1993. "The 1933 World Economic Conference as an Instance of Failed International Cooperation." In *Double-Edged Diplomacy,* edited by Harold Jacobson, Peter Evans, and Robert Putnam, pp. 171–206. University of California Press.

Frankel, Jeffrey A. 1999. "No Single Currency Regime Is Right for All Countries or at All Times." *Princeton Studies in International Finance* 215 (August). International Finance Section, Department of Economics, Princeton University.

Frankel, Jeffrey, and Katherine Rockett. 1988. "International Economic Policy Coordination When Policymakers Do Not Agree on the True Model." *American Economic Review* 78 (June): 318–40.

Giavazzi, Francesco, and Alberto Giovannini. 1989. *Limiting Exchange Rate Flexibility: The European Monetary System.* MIT Press.

Giovannini, Alberto. 1989. "How Fixed Exchange Rate Regimes Work." In *Blueprints for Exchange Rate Management,* edited by Marcus Miller, Barry Eichengreen, and Richard Portes, pp. 13–43. Academic Press.

Goldstein, Morris. 1998. *The Asian Financial Crisis.* Washington: Institute for International Economics.

———. 2002. *Managed Floating Plus.* Washington: Institute for International Economics.

Hernandez, Leonardo, and Peter Montiel. 2003. "Post-Crisis Exchange Rate Policies in Five Asian Countries: Filling in the 'Hollow Middle'?" *Journal of the Japanese and International Economies* 17 (September): 336–69.

Kwan, C. H. 2001. *Yen Bloc: Toward Economic Integration in Asia.* Brookings Institution Press.

Lyons, Richard, and Michael Moore. 2005. "An Information Approach to International Currencies." Working Paper 11220. Cambridge, Mass.: National Bureau of Economic Research (March).

McKinnon, Ronald I. 2005. *Exchange Rates under the East Asian Dollar Standard.* MIT Press.

Pagano, Marco, and Ernst-Ludwig von Thadden. 2004. "The European Bond Markets under EMU." Working Paper 126. Salerno, Italy: Center for Studies in Economics and Finance, University of Salerno (October).

Reinhart, Carmen, and Vincent Reinhart. 2003. "What Hurts Most? G-3 Exchange Rate or Interest Rate Volatility?" In *Economic and Financial Crises in Emerging Market Economies,* edited by Martin Feldstein, pp. 133–66. University of Chicago Press.

Sachs, Jeffrey, and Andrew Warner. 1995. "Economic Reform and the Process of Global Integration." *BPEA*, no. 1: 1–118.

Truman, Edwin, and Anna Wong. 2006. "The Case for an International Reserve Diversification Standard." Working Paper WP05-6. Washington: Institute for International Economics (May).

2 MASARU YOSHITOMI

Global Imbalances and East Asian Monetary Cooperation

At the dawn of the new millennium, East Asia is confronted by both challenges and opportunities.[1] Among the challenges is identifying what role the region should play in resolving the current pattern of global imbalances characterized by both the huge current account deficit of the United States and the vast accumulation of foreign reserves by Asian monetary authorities. Among the opportunities is the chance to use the problem of global imbalances as an occasion to facilitate the closer coordination of monetary and exchange rate policies and design a set of institutions suited to this task.

This chapter explains how these two issues—global imbalances and Asian monetary and financial cooperation—are connected with each other. The second section starts with a description of the global financial landscape and its 800-pound gorilla, the problem of global imbalances. The third section then analyzes the sustainability of the U.S. deficit under different assumptions about prospective rates of return on U.S. net foreign liabilities. The fourth section considers the other side of the coin: namely, the sustainability of East Asia's rapid rate of reserve accumulation. The fifth and sixth sections ask what the United States and East Asia can do to help resolve the global imbalances problem. The final section asks whether the need for collective policy

1. This chapter takes East Asia as including the five major ASEAN countries (Indonesia, Malaysia, the Philippines, Singapore, and Thailand) plus China, Japan, and South Korea.

responses to the current situation will provide further impetus for monetary and financial cooperation in East Asia.

The New International Financial Landscape

The United States is running a current account deficit approaching 7 percent of GDP, an unprecedented ratio for a large, high-income country. This U.S. deficit is absorbing some two-thirds of the net foreign saving of the rest of the world. Major counterparts of this U.S. deficit have been the external surpluses of the East Asian countries, which collectively account for about 45 percent of the sum of world current account surpluses and 55 percent of the U.S. deficit.[2] Asia is thus a key source of finance for the U.S. deficit, and the United States is an important destination for Asia's savings (see table 2-1).

The explosive growth of the U.S. current account deficit dates to the second half of the 1990s. To be sure, the United States had run deficits before, but never at anything approaching their recent magnitude. Initially, the expansion of the U.S. deficit was driven by the surge in private investment associated with enthusiasm for the so-called "New Economy" and the boom in high-tech stocks. Following the collapse of the Nasdaq bubble in 2000–01, the growth of the current account deficit accelerated, in part because of the sharp shift in the fiscal balance from a surplus of some 2 percent of GDP to a deficit approaching 4 percent of GDP.[3] The household saving rate declined more or less continuously from 1997 to the present. Evidently, high private investment, low private saving, and low public saving all contributed to the growth of America's negative saving-investment balance.

To date, the emergence of this deficit has not been associated with sustained movements in the dollar in either direction. From 1997 through 2001, private capital inflows more than sufficed to finance the U.S. current account, and the real effective exchange rate of the dollar appreciated by 17 percent. Since 2002, in contrast, private inflows have fallen short of the amounts needed to finance

2. The regionwide distribution of the U.S. trade deficit of $767 billion in 2005 indicates that the East Asian total, including Japan, accounted for about 45 percent ($348 billion) of the U.S. deficit. Nearly 60 percent of this figure ($202 billion) was China's bilateral trade surplus with the United States—although China's global current account surplus was $159 billion (see discussion that follows). For comparison, exports from the United States to Europe were $186 billion, imports to the United States from Europe were $309 billion, and Europe's bilateral trade balance with the United States was $122 billion.

3. Economists disagree on the extent to which the increase in the fiscal deficit mapped into the increase in the current account deficit. For a flavor of this debate, see Gruber and Kamin (2005) and International Monetary Fund (2005).

Table 2-1. *U.S. and East Asian Global and Bilateral Trade Balances, 2005*
Billions of U.S. dollars

Country or region	*Exports from the United States*	*Imports to the United States*	*Bilateral trade balance with the United States*	*Global current account balance*
Japan	55	138	83	164
China	42	244	202	159
Crisis-hit economies				
Indonesia	3	12	9	3
Malaysia	11	34	23	20
Philippines	7	9	2	3
South Korea	28	44	16	17
Thailand	7	20	13	–4
Non-crisis economies				
Hong Kong	16	9	–7	19
Singapore	21	15	–6	34
Taiwan	22	35	13	16
East Asia total, including Japan	212	560	348	431
U.S. total with the rest of the world	904	1,671	–767	–805

Source: U.S. Census Bureau, "Foreign Trade Statistics," www.census.gov/foreign-trade/balance/index.html; and World Economic Outlook database, April 2006.

the current account, and between January 2002 and December 2004 the real effective exchange rate of the dollar gave back its previous gains, falling by 17 percent. At the end of this cycle, the dollar was back more or less where it started. Rather remarkably, it was essentially back at its average value for the prior quarter century, measured on a real effective basis (see figure 2-1).[4]

Mirroring the deterioration in the U.S. current account balance after 1997, current account balances in East Asia have moved from deficit to surplus (in the case of the crisis-afflicted economies) or from modest surplus to larger surplus (in the case of non-crisis countries). Investment rates in the region fell significantly following the Asian crisis, as capital-impaired banks and firms sought to repair their balance sheets by reducing new lending and borrowing,

4. This feature stands in contrast to the pre-Plaza Accord period (before 1985), when the dollar had clearly become overvalued.

Figure 2-1. *U.S. Investment, Savings, Budget Deficit, Current Account Deficit, and Effective Exchange Rate of the Dollar, 1980–2006*[a]

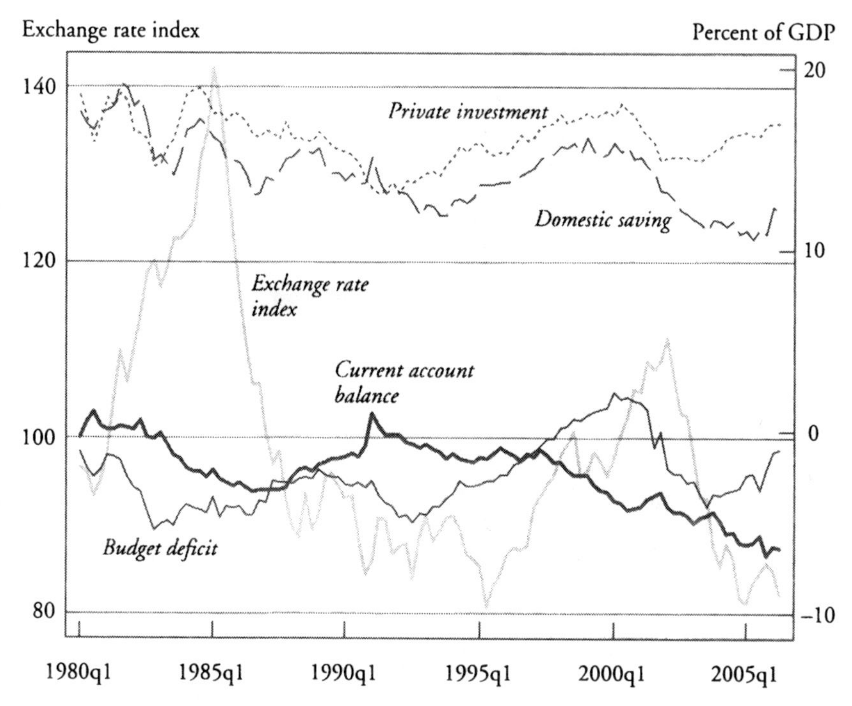

Sources: FRED® (Federal Reserve Economic Data), Federal Reserve Bank of St. Louis, 2006. U.S. Department of Commerce, Bureau of Economic Analysis, for the time series of GDP, gross private savings, gross private investment, federal government budget deficit, and current account balance. Board of Governors of the Federal Reserve System for trade-weighted exchange index of the U.S. dollar, 1973 = 100.

a. Trade weighted exchange index, 1973 = 100 is the weighted average of the daily foreign exchange value of the U.S. dollar against a subset of the broad index of currencies that circulate widely outside the country of issue. Major currency indexes include the euro area, Canada, Japan, United Kingdom, Switzerland, Australia, and Sweden. The trend of trade weighted exchange index of the U.S. dollar is scaled on the left vertical axis, while other series are scaled in percent of GDP on the right vertical axis.

allowing substantial current account surpluses to emerge.[5] Interestingly, this was equally true of the non-crisis countries; even Asian economies like Singapore and Taiwan that were largely immune from the crisis saw their current account surpluses widen after 1997–98. Only in China have investment rates largely kept up with savings rates, limiting the growth of the current account surplus—at least until recently (table 2-2).

Currencies in the crisis-hit East Asian economies, after falling by 50 percent or more as a result of the crisis, have been maintained at levels averaging some

5. Rajan Raghuram, "Perspectives on Global Imbalances" (www.imf.org [January 23, 2006]).

Table 2-2. *Domestic Saving, Capital Formation, and Resource Gap, before and after the Crisis*

Percent of GDP

	Gross domestic saving				*Gross capital formation*				*Saving-investment gap*			
	Pre-crisis		*Post-crisis*		*Pre-crisis*		*Post-crisis*		*Pre-crisis*		*Post-crisis*	
Country	*1990*	*1995*	*2000*	*2003*	*1990*	*1995*	*2000*	*2003*	*1990*	*1995*	*2000*	*2003*
China	38.7	42.5	39	42.7	34.7	40.8	36.3	44.4	4	1.7	2.6	–1.7
Hong Kong	35.2	29.1	31.7	31.6	27.5	34.7	28.1	22.6	7.6	–5.5	3.6	8.7
Indonesia	32.3	30.6	25.6	21.5	30.7	31.9	16.1	16	1.5	–1.3	9.5	5.5
Malaysia	34.4	39.7	47.2	42.9	32.4	43.6	27.2	21.8	2	–3.9	20	21.1
Philippines	18.7	14.5	17.3	20.1	24.2	22.5	21.2	18.7	–5.5	–7.9	–3.9	1.4
Singapore	43.3	50.2	47.9	46.7	36.4	34.2	32	13.4	6.9	16.1	15.9	33.3
South Korea	37.2	36.5	33.9	32.8	37.7	37.7	31	29.4	–0.5	–1.1	2.9	3.4
Taiwan	27.6	25.9	24.4	23.5	23.1	25.3	22.9	17.2	4.5	0.6	1.5	6.3
Thailand	34.3	37.3	33.2	33.1	41.4	42.1	22.8	25.2	–7.1	–4.8	10.4	7.9

Source: Key indicators, Asian Development Bank.

15 to 20 percent below pre-crisis levels (as shown in figure 2-2). This has been accomplished through central bank intervention in foreign exchange markets. While the exchange rates of the non-crisis economies have been more stable, there has been an analogous attempt to employ foreign exchange market intervention to limit currency appreciation as the pace of expansion accelerates. The extreme case is China, which kept the renminbi fixed at 8.27 to the dollar from 1994 until July 20, 2005, when it permitted a revaluation of 2.1 percent—ushering in a very limited increase in flexibility.

The objectives of Asian central banks in accumulating large quantities of reserves include insuring themselves against another capital account crisis and maintaining competitive exchange rates to support the export-oriented thrust of economic growth.[6] The first objective was more important in the immediate aftermath of the crisis, while the second has arguably dominated thinking in policy circles in recent years.

The Sustainability of the U.S. Deficit

The question for the future is whether this pattern of global imbalances, involving both large deficits in the United States and extensive reserve accumulation in Asia, can be sustained.

The answer hinges on how one interprets the financial implications. As the United States runs current account deficits, it accumulates debt against the rest of the world. One way of analyzing the sustainability of its deficits is thus to calculate how much U.S. debt must eventually be held in the portfolios of international investors. This analysis should take into account the evolution of interest rates and risk premiums on the U.S. liabilities held by international investors, as well as the expected rate of growth of U.S. GDP.

A useful starting point, following Mussa (2004), is the following simple equation for the long-run equilibrium value of U.S. net liabilities relative to U.S. GDP:

$$n^* = c\ /\ (g - r), \qquad (2\text{-}1)$$

where n^* is the long-run ratio of net external debt relative to GDP, c is the current account deficit relative to GDP, g is the nominal growth rate of the

6. These two motivations are labeled "precautionary" and "mercantilist" by Aizenman and Lee (2005).

Figure 2-2. *Real Effective Exchange Rates in Asia, 2000 = 100*

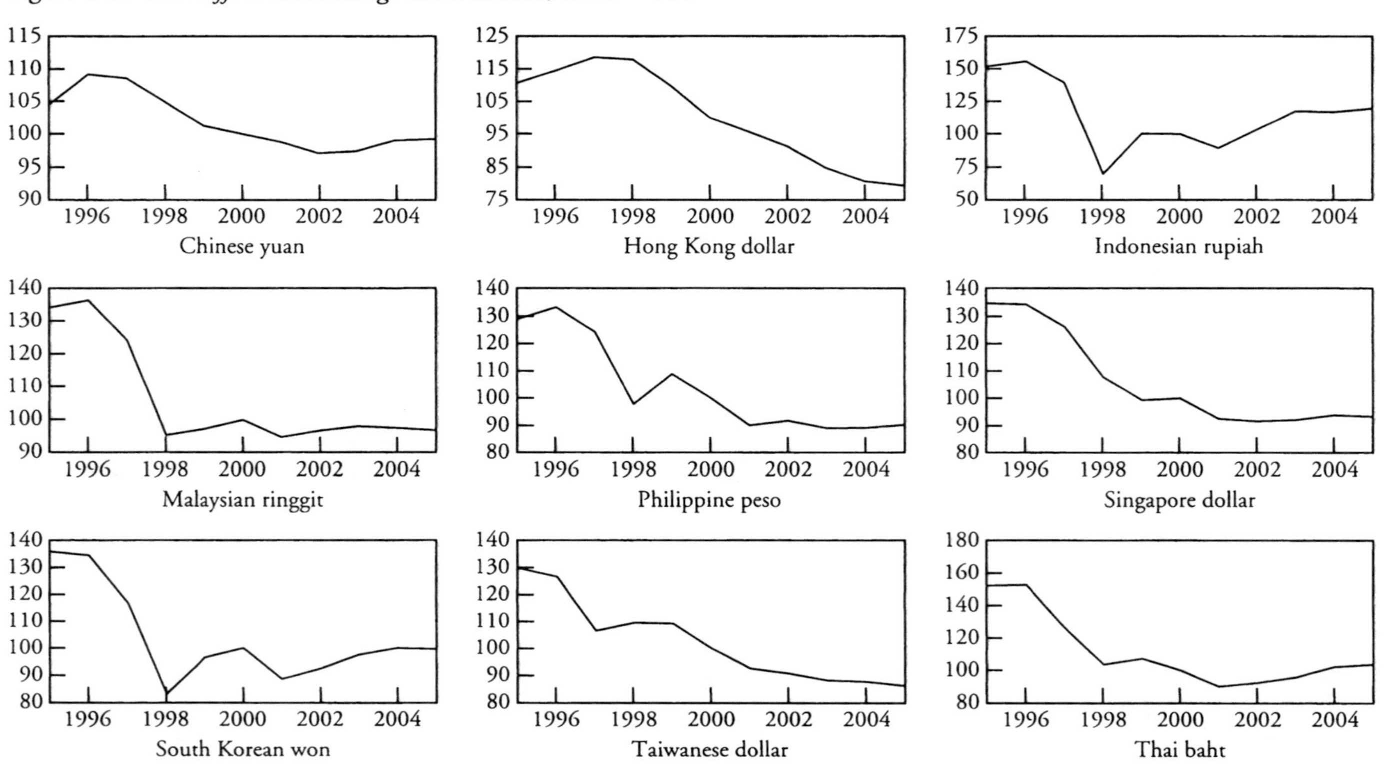

Source: CEPII-CHELEM database.

economy, and r is the nominal rate of return on net external debt.[7] Assuming that U.S. current account deficits continue to run in the range of 6 percent of GDP, that the underlying rate of growth of nominal GDP in the United States equals 5 percent, and that rate of return on net foreign liabilities remains negligible, as it is now (for more on this assumption, see the discussion that follows), equation 2-1 implies that net external debt will eventually reach 120 percent of U.S. GDP, a much higher level than ever witnessed for a large advanced industrial country.

Indeed, under these assumptions net external debt will have already reached 64 percent of GDP after only 10 years (see table 2-3). U.S. net liabilities of 64 percent of U.S. GDP would represent 19 percent of the financial wealth of other countries. At one level this is not especially alarming. It is quite plausible that investors might willingly hold financial claims on the United States of this magnitude. Highly innovative U.S. financial markets are good at creating financial instruments that foreign investors find attractive to add to their portfolios.[8] In addition, the fact that the U.S. dollar is a key currency creates an additional demand for dollar-denominated assets on the part of the rest of the world. This assumes, of course, that nothing happens to cast doubt on the ability and willingness of the United States to service those obligations or to change the dollar's status as an international currency.[9]

As a modest step in the direction of greater realism, such calculations should take into account the fact that the rate of return on U.S. net external liabilities (r) may evolve unfavorably for the United States. At the moment, the realized rate of return on U.S. foreign debt is strikingly low relative to the realized return on U.S. foreign assets.[10] Despite the fact that U.S. net external liabilities amounted to 29 percent of GDP in 2004, net international investment income remained slightly positive for the United States. Hence the rate of return on net foreign liabilities remained negative, buttressing the sustainability of the U.S. external debt. One factor explaining this return differential is the fact that U.S. assets abroad are largely in the form of equities (including foreign direct investment), while U.S. external liabilities are largely in the form of fixed income

7. For purposes of empirical implementation, the net nominal interest rate r is defined as net international investment income divided by net U.S. external debt. Net international investment income is the difference between international income received on gross U.S. assets held abroad and that paid on gross U.S. external debt.

8. This point has been emphasized by Caballero, Fahri, and Gourinchas (2006).

9. For more discussion of this, see also chapter 3 by Yu and chapter 5 by Kawai later in this volume.

10. As emphasized by Gourinchas and Rey (2005), Hausmann and Sturzenegger (2005), and Kitchen (2006).

Table 2-3. *Share of U.S. Assets in the Portfolios of Investors from the Rest of the World (ROW)*[a]

Unit as indicated

	2004		*2014*		*Eventually*[b]	
U.S. assets	*United States*	*ROW*	*United States*	*ROW*	*United States*	*ROW*
Own total financial assets, gross (trillions of U.S.$)	36	40	62	69	. . .	. . .
Percent of U.S. GDP	300	333	300	333	300	333
External assets, gross (trillions of U.S.$)	9.5	12	16.2	29.6	. . .	. . .
Percent of U.S. GDP	78	100	78	142	78	198
Percent of its own financial assets	26	30	26	43	26	60
Net external assets (NEA) (trillions of U.S.$)	–2.5	2.5	–13.2	13.2	. . .	. . .
					If net interest rate on NEA = 0%	
Percent of U.S. GDP	–21	21	64	64	120	120
Percent of its own financial assets	7	6	21	19	40	36
					If net interest rate on NEA = 1%	
Percent of U.S. GDP					150	150
Percent of its own financial assets					50	45
					If net interest rate on NEA = 2%	
Percent of U.S. GDP					200	200
Percent of its own financial assets					67	60

Sources: U.S. Bureau of Economic Analysis, 2006, "International Investment Position" (www.bea.gov); Blanchard, Giavazzi, and Sa (2005); Edwards (2005).

a. Assumptions: $c = 6$ percent, $g = 5$ percent; U.S. wealth = 300 percent of U.S. GDP; ROW wealth = 333 percent of U.S. GDP; U.S. and ROW wealth grow at the same rate; percentage of U.S. wealth in foreign assets = 26 percent. Financial wealth is defined as net financial assets and excludes tangible assets such as real estate and durable goods.

b. Eventual net external debt/GDP = $c/(g - r)$, where c = current account deficit/GDP, g = nominal growth rate of the economy, and r = nominal interest rate on net external debt.

assets (including Treasury bills purchased by foreign central banks).[11] In other words, the average return received by U.S. investors (3.9 percent in 2004) exceeds the average return received by foreign investors (2.6 percent) because the United States is holding riskier assets. But this fact that U.S. foreign investments are riskier than foreign investments in the United States also suggests that there could be a period when the income on U.S. foreign investments could collapse, with unfavorable implications for the interest-income component of the country's balance of payments.

Even if the United States has enjoyed a negative *r* until now, this is unlikely to remain the case as investors in the rest of the world accumulate more U.S. liabilities. In order to add more U.S. assets to their portfolios, they will demand a higher rate of return.[12] And as *r* turns against the United States, any level of net external indebtedness will become more burdensome.

All such calculations are sensitive to the assumptions imposed with regard to growth rates, interest rates, and other variables. This makes it important to explore their sensitivity with respect to alternative parameter values. Table 2-3 therefore explores a number of alternative scenarios for the evolution of the rate of return on U.S. net foreign assets and the country's debt/GDP ratio. Assuming that the net rate of return moves from the negative values that have prevailed historically to zero, a 6 percent of GDP current account deficit translates into a net foreign debt that is 64 percent of U.S. GDP and 64 percent of rest-of-world GDP in ten years, as noted. In long-run equilibrium, these ratios reach nearly twice that level. As a share of the financial assets of the rest of the world, claims on the United States rise to 19 percent in 2014 (from 6 percent today) and 36 percent in the long-run steady state. If the U.S. is required to pay a modest 1 percent rate of return on its net foreign liabilities, then the debt/GDP ratio would rise to 150 percent, and foreign investors would have to hold 45 percent of their financial assets in claims on the United States. If the net rate of return rises to 2 percent, these numbers soar to 200 percent and 60 percent, respectively (table 2-3).

It is implausible that even the additional demand for U.S. assets that derives from the dollar's key currency status would suffice to induce foreign investors to hold such large shares of their total wealth in U.S. assets without receiving a much higher rate of return. But that higher rate of return would make it correspondingly more difficult for the United States to service its external debt. This is the crux of the sustainability problem.

11. This is why Gourinchas and Rey (2005) refer to the United States as venture capitalist to the world. In addition, Gourinchas and Rey show that the United States earns a somewhat higher return within each category of assets (equities, bonds, foreign direct investment, and the like).

12. See Roubini and Setser (2004).

On the other hand, if the United States current account deficit could somehow be reduced to less than 3 percent of U.S. GDP, then the U.S. external debt ratio would remain below 60 percent of U.S. GDP and 15 percent of the financial wealth of the rest of the world. This is a more plausible scenario, and it underlies the consensus forecast that the U.S. deficit will have to be cut by half.

The Sustainability of East Asian Reserve Accumulation

Foreign reserve accumulation by Asian monetary authorities has been an important source of finance for the U.S. current account deficit since the beginning of the current decade. Reserve accumulation serves to keep Asian currencies from appreciating against the dollar, but it also has a variety of other, unintended consequences. It increases base money and thereby generates excess liquidity in the banking system. In turn this raises the money supply and fans inflation. To limit these adverse effects, East Asian central banks have engaged in extensive sterilization, selling government bonds or central bank bills for cash to keep the monetary base unchanged and seeking to mop up excess liquidity in the banking system.

So far these sterilization policies have largely succeeded in preventing rates of money supply growth from accelerating excessively. National rates of inflation as measured by the increase in the CPI have remained low (tables 2-4 and 2-5). However, there are difficulties with sterilization operations, which threaten to grow more serious with time. As a result of the sterilization of external surpluses, commercial banks end up holding central bank bills yielding low interest rates. This erodes bank profitability and undermines the efficiency of credit allocation by the banking system. In addition, sterilization grows more costly as the stock of central bank bills or government securities grows large and investors demand higher interest rates on these instruments. Higher interest rates may also have the perverse effect of attracting additional capital inflows, requiring yet additional sterilization, and launching public finances onto a vicious spiral.

In addition, the continued accumulation of U.S. Treasury securities may result in an inefficient allocation of resources insofar as the same resources could instead be devoted to private and public investment. The same economic capacity that is being used to produce exports destined for the U.S. market and the same income that is being salted away in the form of dollar reserves could instead be used to underwrite investments in housing, water supply, roads, and infrastructure generally, not to mention education and health care for Asian populations.

Finally, the accumulation of dollar-denominated assets exposes East Asian monetary authorities to capital losses if the dollar falls. This creates a dilemma for regional central banks, as discussed in the next to last section of this chapter.

Adjustment Policies for the United States

How should the United States respond to its unsustainable external imbalances? Boosting saving is clearly preferable to reducing investment. Boosting national saving would involve fiscal consolidation to raise public saving (more precisely, to reduce public dis-saving) and raising interest rates to dampen asset markets and limit the rate of growth of household consumption (the dominant explanation for the very low household savings rates in the United States is the tendency for families to take equity out of their increasingly valuable homes). There is an obvious danger, however, that such policies would be recessionary.[13] Hence the reduction in domestic absorption should be matched by an increase in net exports in order to keep the engines of U.S. industry humming.

A dollar depreciation, which would enhance the competitiveness of U.S. exports, would assist this aspect of the adjustment process. It would help reconcile the need for the maintenance of both internal and external balance by assigning two instruments (expenditure switching and expenditure reducing policies) to these two objectives. In contrast, dollar depreciation alone, without any accompanying absorption reducing policies, would only fan inflation. In this scenario, nominal depreciation of the dollar would not result in a real depreciation, since excess demand would only push up prices accordingly. Hence expenditure switching would be frustrated as well. Of course, there is another scenario in which the Federal Reserve System grows anxious about accelerating inflation and raises interest rates sharply, or in which foreign investors grow impatient with the absence of U.S. adjustment and pull the plug, causing U.S. Treasury bond prices to fall and market interest rates to rise. In this scenario, higher interest rates would compress U.S. investment, bringing about the necessary change in the level of expenditure—but in a less desirable way.

Thus the optimal policy mix for the United States would involve fiscal consolidation combined with dollar depreciation. Assuming that steps are taken to raise public and private saving, the dollar would have to depreciate by some

13. This is why the Federal Reserve Board has insisted in raising interest rates gradually and normalizing monetary conditions at a "measured pace."

Table 2-4. *Money Supply, Annual Growth Rates, China, Malaysia, South Korea, and Thailand, 2000–05*

Percent

	China		*Malaysia*				*South Korea*				*Thailand*			
Year	*M1*	*M2*	*M1*	*M2*	*M3*	*M0*	*M1*	*M2*	*M3*	*M0*	*M1*	*M2*	*M3*	*M0*
2000	19.80	16.10	17.08	7.36	5.22	7.42	24.30	2.70	5.76	9.71	10.41	1.85	2.73	12.66
2001	14.03	13.66	6.37	4.04	4.69	4.34	18.65	7.04	9.46	12.00	8.39	5.51	5.71	8.03
2002	15.69	15.51	11.24	5.28	5.72	8.11	23.49	11.43	13.31	9.85	12.30	4.35	3.22	11.13
2003	19.19	19.98	10.73	8.58	8.31	9.84	6.55	7.49	8.22	4.81	14.88	2.39	3.57	11.62
2004	16.52	16.25	14.62	15.17	10.45	9.08	8.22	4.39	5.86	3.13	13.60	6.60	6.42	11.16
2005[a]	12.10	14.12	12.96	25.38	12.73	5.68	6.56	4.92	3.83	1.05	11.46	4.70	5.70	9.42

Source: Datastream.

a. January–March 2005.

Table 2-5. *Inflation, Annual Rates of Consumer, Producer, and Stock Price Increase, China, Malaysia, South Korea, and Thailand, 2000–04*

Percent

	China			*Malaysia*			*South Korea*			*Thailand*		
Year	*PPI*	*CPI*	*Shanghai securities*[a]	*PPI*	*CPI*	*Share prices*	*PPI*	*CPI*	*Share prices*	*PPI*	*CPI*	*Share prices*
2000	1.4	1.4	55.2	–3.8	1.5	–26.3	–0.1	3.2	–48.8	3.6	1.4	–41.5
2001	–5.7	–2.2	–17.4	–1.9	1.1	1.1	–2.6	3.1	23.3	0.8	0.7	4.0
2002	6.7	1.4	11.2	12.1	1.6	–6.3	2.7	3.7	–15.7	4.9	2.1	12.7
2003	1.1	2.8	7.9	2.6	1.0	21.8	3.7	3.3	29.3	2.8	1.3	72.7
2004	2.2	–1.3	–23.9	3.5	2.4	12.4	4.0	3.1	6.6	8.2	2.6	–8.5

Source: Datastream.

a. Annual change in the market value of the Shanghai Stock Exchange (in current prices).

30 percent on a real effective basis over a period of a few years to crowd in the requisite quantity of exports and reduce the current account deficit to 3 percent of GDP.

East Asia's Role in Resolving the Current Global Imbalances

How should East Asian countries prepare for the prospect of a 30 percent real effective depreciation of the dollar?[14] Most obviously, they can cooperate in preventing the dollar's fall from disturbing the pattern of intraregional exchange rates. This is desirable for several reasons. First, since intraregional trade accounts for about 55 percent of East Asia's total trade, concerted increases in the value of East Asian currencies against the dollar would attenuate effective exchange rate changes in the region. In turn this would mitigate the recessionary impact when Asian currencies appreciate against the dollar.

In addition, coordinating the adjustment of Asian currencies against the dollar would support the further elaboration of regional production and distribution networks, since more stable intraregional exchange rates are more likely to foster intraregional trade.[15] In contrast, there is a risk that these networks might be disturbed were the dollar's fall allowed to precipitate large changes in intraregional exchange rates. Stable exchange rates within the region would also be conducive to the maintenance of intraregional flows of foreign direct investment (FDI), which have been so important to the development of these production chains in recent years.

Finally, if Asian governments and central banks agree on moving together, there would be a solution to the prisoner's-dilemma problem where no country allows its currency to rise against the dollar because its neighbors and competitors prevent their currencies from rising against the dollar. The "sustainability arithmetic" laid out above suggests that some appreciation of Asian currencies against the dollar is inevitable. If this is delayed because of the prisoner's dilemma, the fall in the dollar will then be larger and more disruptive when it ultimately comes.[16]

The context for these observations, as already noted, is the growing economic interdependence of the East Asia region. Intraregional trade is large and

14. This is the academic consensus of the magnitude of the remaining adjustment. See for example Obstfeld and Rogoff (2004); Blanchard, Giavazzi, and Sa (2005).

15. The magnitude of the negative effect of exchange rate volatility on trade (and, by implication, the trade-creating effects of exchange rate stability) is disputed by economists; the literature is described and some additional evidence is presented by Shin and Wang in chapter 4 below.

16. The ultimate fall will be larger because it will be necessary to crowd in additional U.S. net exports in order to service a larger U.S. external debt. It will be more disruptive insofar as large exchange rate

expanding rapidly (see table 2-6). Much of that trade, notably the portion in parts and components, derives from intricate production and distribution networks that increasingly bind together regional economies. Intraregional FDI flows have worked to reinforce the development of these networks. The classic example is how Japan, South Korea, Taiwan, and multinational corporations operating in various ASEAN countries produce sophisticated technology-intensive intermediate and capital goods that are then shipped to China for assembly by low-wage workers, with the finished products then exported to markets throughout the world. Recent data show that these processed exports now account for fully 55 percent of China's total exports (see table 2-7). In turn the lion's share of China's processed exports, on the order of 80 percent, is supplied by foreign investment enterprises: that is, enterprises financed in substantial part by FDI, often from neighboring Asian countries.

Trade within these networks is referred to as vertical intra-industry trade (VIIT). VIIT differs both from the inter-industry trade described in the textbooks, which involves the exchange of capital-intensive and labor-intensive final goods between North and South, and the traditional forms of intra-industry trade described by trade theorists: that is, the exchange between different developed countries of two different varieties of the same category of goods (such as automobiles). VIIT allows the production processes of an industry (such as consumer electronics) to be split into fragmented production blocks that can then be situated in different countries. Production blocks are allocated across developing, emerging, and developed economies based on comparative advantage as determined by relative endowments of capital, skill, and labor and by physical and institutional infrastructure.[17] VIIT has led to large efficiency gains and helped to make East Asia the manufacturing center of the world. It has also fostered growing interdependence within the region, making individual countries' exchange rate policies a matter of regional concern.

Because of the importance of these trading networks, Chinese value added in processed exports is small, on the order of 20 percent. In other words, the bulk of the value of Chinese exports represents intermediate inputs imported from the rest of Asia. This means that a unilateral revaluation of the renminbi would not have a major effect on the cost of Chinese exports to the rest of the world and hence on China's current account surplus and the problem of global

changes are more likely to catch hedge funds and other investors wrong-footed and will be difficult for the financial system to absorb.

17. Analytical treatments of the phenomenon include Chang and Chen (1994) and, more recently, Lambertini (2004).

Table 2-6. *Intraregional Trade Share, Various Regions, 1993–2004*[a]

Percent

Regions	*1993*	*1995*	*1997*	*1999*	*2000*	*2001*	*2002*	*2003*	*2004*
East Asia-14, including Japan[b]	46.0	49.9	49.3	47.4	50.1	48.5	50.6	51.6	51.9
Emerging East Asia-13[b]	31.8	34.9	36.4	35.3	36.6	35.8	38.3	39.0	39.3
NIEs-4	14.5	15.3	15.4	14.7	15.4	14.7	15.2	14.5	14.4
ASEAN-9[b]	20.0	21.8	21.7	22.2	23.5	22.3	23.1	22.6	22.6
NAFTA[c]	42.2	42.9	45.6	48.3	49.0	48.7	48.2	47.1	46.4
European Union-15[d]	62.8	63.5	62.0	62.4	60.1	60.1	60.5	61.1	60.9

Source: CEPII-CHELEM database.

a. The intraregional trade share is defined as: $X_{ii}/[(X_{i\cdot} + X_{\cdot i})/2]$, where X_{ii} represents exports of region *i* to region *i*, X_i is total exports of region *i* to the world, and $X_{\cdot i}$ is total exports of the world to region *i*.

b. East Asia-14 includes emerging East Asia-13 and Japan. Emerging East Asia-13 includes the Asian Newly Industrialized Econmies (NIEs) (Hong Kong, Singapore, South Korea, and Taiwan), eight ASEAN members (Brunei, Cambodia, Indonesia, Laos, Malaysia, the Philippines, Thailand, and Vietnam), and China. ASEAN-9 includes Singapore. Trade data for Myanmar are not available.

c. NAFTA includes the United States, Canada, and Mexico.

d. EU-15 includes Austria, Belgium, Denmark, Finland, France, Germany, Greece, Ireland, Luxembourg, Netherlands, Italy, Portugal, Spain, Sweden, and United Kingdom.

imbalances. Moreover, the fact that China imports sophisticated intermediate goods from East Asia more than from the United States, while exporting final products to markets around the world, including the United States, implies that bilateral trade imbalances between China and the United States would remain large even if China's global trade surplus disappeared.[18]

The effects of the joint appreciation of the whole set of East Asian currencies against the dollar would be different. In this case there would be a change in the relative dollar price not merely of Chinese value added but of Chinese output (under the simplifying assumption that all inputs into Chinese assembly operations come from neighboring East Asian countries).[19] In this scenario one can imagine a much larger swing in both Asian and U.S. current account balances and a more decisive resolution of the global imbalances problem.

But this joint appreciation will not occur automatically. Since different Asian countries produce and export different mixes of products, depreciation of the dollar against local currencies will have different effects on the competitiveness of different economies in the region. More developed East Asian countries export large amounts of technology-intensive capital and intermediate goods, while the region's less developed countries export large amounts of low-skill–intensive consumer goods. Hence there is a complementary relationship between China and less developed Asia on the one hand and more developed Asia on the other hand in sophisticated intermediate and capital goods trade. Similarly, there is a complementary relationship between China and multinational corporations operating in ASEAN that export sophisticated technology-intensive parts and components there for processing. In contrast, there is a largely competitive relationship between China and less developed Asian countries in labor-intensive consumer goods trade.

Even if all Asian countries are affected in broadly similar ways, there may still be a collective action problem hindering a concerted response. Any one country that resists the call for joint appreciation will steal a competitive advantage, and the knowledge that neighboring countries and rivals will be reluctant to allow the appreciation of their currencies may stymie efforts to engineer any appreciation at all. The result would be a coordination failure: while all countries would be better off if their currencies were allowed to appreciate together, since this would contribute to an orderly resolution of global imbalances, no

18. In 2005, the U.S. bilateral trade deficit vis-à-vis China was $200 billion, compared to a U.S. current account deficit against the world of $800 billion. China's overall current account surplus, by comparison, was $160 billion (table 2-2). Again it follows that it is inappropriate to demand a unilateral renminbi appreciation simply because America's bilateral deficit with China is large.

19. In reality, some 70 percent of those inputs into Chinese assembly operations come from neighboring Asian countries, as shown in table 2-7.

Table 2-7. *China's Processing Trade, 1993 and 2004*

Percent unless otherwise noted

Imports/exports	*World*	*South Korea and Taiwan*	*Japan*	*ASEAN 5*	*Hong Kong*	*United States*	*EU-15*	*Rest of world*
Imports								
1993								
Total imports	100	18	22	6	10	10	15	19
Normal imports	37	2	8	3	1	5	8	9
Imports for processing	35	11	8	2	7	2	2	3
Others	28	5	7	1	2	3	6	5
2004								
Total imports	100	23	17	11	2	8	12	28
Normal imports	44	6	6	4	1	4	8	15
Imports for processing	40	14	7	5	1	2	4	7
Others	16	3	4	2	0	2	1	5
Exports								
1993								
Total exports	100	5	17	5	24	18	13	18
Normal exports	47	2	10	4	10	6	7	9
Processed exports	48	2	7	1	14	13	7	4
Others	5	0	0	0	0	0	0	5

2004								
Total exports	100	7	12	6	17	21	17	19
Normal exports	41	3	5	3	4	6	7	13
Processed exports	55	4	7	3	12	14	10	5
Others	4	0	0	0	1	1	0	2
Balance of trade (U.S. $billions)								
1993								
Balance of trade	−12.2	−14.0	−7.5	−1.3	11.6	6.3	−3.5	−3.8
Normal trade	5.2	0.3	0.7	−0.1	7.7	0.0	−2.0	−1.5
Processing trade	7.9	−9.5	−1.3	−0.6	5.7	9.7	4.2	−0.3
Others	−25.2	−4.9	−6.9	−0.6	−1.7	−3.4	−5.8	−1.9
2004								
Balance of trade	32	−85.6	−20.8	−22.9	89.1	80.3	31.8	−39.9
Normal trade	45.9	−14.7	−5.7	−2.9	19.9	13.7	−2.0	37.6
Processing trade	106.3	−54.9	3.3	−11.7	64.3	72.7	37.5	−5.0
Others	−69.7	−16.0	−18.4	−8.3	4.9	−6.2	−3.7	−21.9

Sources: Gaulier, Lemoine, and Unal-Kesencis (2005); China's customs statistics; author's calculations.

one country would be willing to move first. In the absence of a mechanism for coordinating their decisions, there may be no movement at all.

One form of concerted action would be for all countries in the region to agree to allow their currencies to appreciate more or less jointly against the dollar by the aforementioned 30 percent. However, a uniform depreciation would not take sufficient account of differences in national circumstances and would ignore the extent of cumulated appreciation since 2002. There is a case that currencies that have not appreciated against the dollar since 2002 should be allowed to catch up with the others. To put it another way, countries that have pioneered the move to greater exchange rate flexibility should not be penalized for having exercised this leadership.

Adjustments of this sort could be achieved more easily if East Asian countries adopted more flexible exchange rate regimes. Ideally, these more flexible regimes would be characterized by two elements: a multiple currency basket-based reference rate instead of a dollar-based central rate; and a wider band around the reference rate. Combining these two elements would provide policymakers with more leeway for managing the speed and magnitude of appreciation while still taking into account differences in national economic conditions. They would allow the region's now more flexible exchange rates to be managed to avoid destabilizing fluctuations.

The current proposal would involve consultation before individual national decisions on the new central rate and the surrounding band, followed by individual action by each central bank to manage the national currency. The idea is decidedly not that the participating countries would commit to a regional set of central rates and fluctuation bands, which would be tantamount to establishing a regional currency grid, in the manner of the European Monetary System established in 1979. Such an arrangement would be overly constraining, given the diversity of economic and financial circumstances in the region. It would be difficult if not impossible to sustain; in particular, the slow development of political solidarity in the region would create doubts among market participants about whether the participating countries were really prepared to support the central rates and fluctuation limits of their neighbors. European experience in the 1990s suggests that, absent such political solidarity and commitment, formally establishing a regional parity grid would only serve to create an engine for further crises.

Some will claim that simply moving to a free float would allow exchange rates to reflect market fundamentals more accurately. But given the shallow and narrow domestic capital markets that exist in many East Asian economies, not least China, a free float would almost certainly result in undesirably high levels of volatility. Banks and firms with limited access to hedging instruments would

Table 2-8. *Exchange Rate Regime Trade-offs*

	Exchange rate regimes			
Policy goals	*Pre-WWI gold standard or currency board*	*Bretton Woods 1945–73*	*Floating since 1973*	*Crawling bands*
Fixing the exchange rate	O	O (but soft peg)	× (sacrificed)	Δ with bands (with regional lender of last resort)
Free capital movements	O	× (sacrificed)	O	Δ with short-term capital controls
Independent monetary policy for low inflation and high employment	× (sacrificed)	O	O	O

Source: Yoshitomi (2004).
Note: O indicates that a policy goal is attainable.
× indicates that a policy goal is sacrificed.
Δ indicates that a policy goal is partly attainable (partly sacrificed).

find it difficult to insure themselves against this volatility. Most observers therefore recommend neither a free float nor a fixed dollar peg but rather greater exchange rate flexibility in the context of a multiple currency basket-based reference rate with a band: that is, a regime that combines some of the best characteristics of fixed and floating rates. This approach is described schematically in table 2-8. If the majority of East Asian countries adopt such regimes, dollar depreciation would tend to produce appreciation across the region without disrupting intraregional exchange rate relationships.

Greater flexibility would benefit China in particular. China is moving to greater capital account openness, if for no other reason than because of the commitments associated with its accession to the World Trade Organization. These commitments require the country to extend free access to foreign banks and other financial institutions engaged in renminbi-based financial activities by the end of 2006. With foreign banks undertaking a range of renminbi-denominated transactions, it is hard to imagine that China will be able to retain strict control of its capital account. In addition the Chinese authorities are taking a variety of other measures to liberalize the capital account gradually, particularly on the outflow side so as to moderate the pressure for appreciation of the renminbi exerted by capital flows.

Given this reality, financial conditions at home and abroad will become increasingly tightly linked, and a more flexible exchange rate, achieved through the adoption of wider fluctuation bands, would enable China to maintain greater autonomy in its monetary policy. Increased flexibility would also give Chinese banks and traders the incentive to invest in managing exchange rate exposure and provide impetus for the more rapid development of forward markets and related financial infrastructure. More proactively, China should purposefully promote the growth of the requisite institutional infrastructure (such as strengthened regulation, prudential supervision, internationally recognized accounting standards, and the development of a true credit culture) so that the economy can accommodate greater exchange rate flexibility in the not-too-distant future. Reassuringly, there are signs that the Chinese authorities recognize the importance of this agenda.

If Asian countries allow their currencies to appreciate, the expenditure switching effects would be recessionary, other things equal. This makes it important that those other things not be allowed to remain equal and that the recessionary impact on aggregate demand be offset by absorption increasing policies. The latter include fiscal and structural policies designed to speed the development of both physical and human infrastructure (particularly in rural areas) and using deregulation to promote competition and productivity growth in the non-tradable sector. These policies could promote production for domestic markets and thus rely more on domestic markets rather than exports to create jobs.

But here too there is a collective action problem. The positive impact on aggregate demand of fiscal expansion tends to spill over to neighboring countries (more so with the development of intraregional trade and investment of the sort previously noted). Given the fiscal conservatism of Asian governments (or, more precisely, most Asian governments), there is a consequent tendency to undersupply the relevant fiscal measures, as each country relies excessively on its regional neighbors for demand support.

A regional forum in which the need for fiscal support was discussed and coordinated would help to solve this further coordination problem. Such a forum would also provide a venue for the development of common understandings regarding the conduct of monetary and exchange rate policies and the need for burden sharing in the adjustment of Asian currencies against the dollar. This would help to solve the first mover problems that would otherwise render Asian governments reluctant to see their currencies appreciate against the dollar and to provide the associated fiscal support for domestic demand.

Asia already possesses plenty of regional forums, from ASEAN to ASEAN+3 to EMEAP (the Executives' Meeting of East Asia-Pacific Central Banks) and APEC (Asia Pacific Economic Cooperation). Why then is the argument for yet another "talk shop"? In a nutshell, none of these existing institutions has the ideal composition and structure to engineer monetary and exchange rate cooperation. ASEAN excludes the three most consequential players: China, Japan, and Korea. While ASEAN+3 corrects this deficiency, it includes five low-income countries whose economic, monetary, and financial circumstances are very different and which would not obviously be party to coordinated monetary and exchange rate adjustments. APEC includes the United States, rendering it an inappropriate vehicle for an East Asian initiative. EMEAP, as an organization of East Asian central banks, is well suited to the task, but includes Australia and New Zealand, which are firmly committed to freely floating exchange rates and whose participation in regional currency coordination is thus in doubt.

Moreover, few of these organizations possess a permanent secretariat with the resources and independence to help frame the common policy and conduct firm surveillance of the participants. A brand new entity could be endowed with this expertise and responsibilities. At this point, the entity in question begins to sound less like a forum for discussion and negotiation than an international organization with agenda setting powers: a proto-Asian Monetary Fund. It may be necessary to contemplate building the foundations for such an institution and taking at least a modest first step in this direction if Asia is serious about regional monetary coordination.

Conclusion

The point of departure for this chapter is the premise that the current constellation of global imbalances cannot be sustained indefinitely. The most important action needed to resolve this problem is for the United States to take steps to increase its domestic saving rate. Absent action on its part, the dollar will depreciate substantially, sooner or later, as foreign investors grow reluctant to absorb additional dollar-denominated assets into their portfolios. This decline could be gradual and benign, but it could also be sudden and disruptive.

Given the importance of the dollar for international financial markets, a sharp fall in its value could wreak havoc with other exchange rates. An increase in the cost of U.S. imports and in the difficulty of selling into the U.S. market will affect different exporting countries in different ways. Sharp changes in asset prices may cause distress for institutional and individual investors, who may have to sell other assets (including other currencies) to raise liquidity. All these are reasons why a sharp fall in the dollar would likely have a significant effect on other bilateral exchange rate relationships. And a sharp increase in volatility in other foreign exchange markets would not have a positive effect on efforts to foster regional integration.

This creates an argument for East Asian countries to work together to keep intraregional exchange rates relatively stable. This would be easiest if countries in the region first move toward the adoption of similar exchange rate regimes. If some continue pegging to the dollar while others float, effective coordination would be much more difficult. If some operate bands vis-à-vis the dollar while others set their central parities relative to a basket of currencies, difficulties would again ensue. An ideal transitional regime would be if all Asian countries used a common basket of currencies to set their reference or central rates and established wide bands around those central parities.

The adoption of more flexible exchange rates throughout the region would have several advantages from the point of view of the coordination of exchange rate policies. If the dollar dropped, there would be no obstacle to the whole group of East Asian currencies' rising against it. The current regime where Hong Kong operates a currency board vis-à-vis the dollar and China continues to limit fluctuations against the dollar raises the specter that some Asian currencies would be prevented from rising against the dollar, which would fan financial tensions in the region and conceivably even frustrate the global adjustment process. In contrast, maintaining the stability of intraregional exchange rates would sustain and foster the continued expansion of intraregional trade and investment, which are increasingly important for the East Asia region.

The appreciation of East Asian currencies against the dollar will slow the growth of exports to the United States, other things equal. Indeed, steps by the United States to import less and export more are the essence of the process of global rebalancing and essential to the restoration of external debt sustainability. This means that currency appreciation should be accompanied by absorption increasing policies in the rest of the world, and in Asia specifically. These would offset the recessionary impact of currency appreciation and also be consistent with the new economic strategy in East Asia of encouraging domestic demand rather than relying excessively on the expansion of net exports.

A combination of absorption increasing and expenditure switching policies would thus be the appropriate policy mix for Asian countries confronted with the problem of global imbalances. Without currency appreciation, policies aimed at increasing domestic demand would produce overheated economies. But without policies to increase domestic demand, currency appreciation by itself would be contractionary. Only by combining these two sets of initiatives could the East Asian economies simultaneously achieve both internal and external balance. And only by coordinating policies in the region is there any likelihood that something resembling the optimal set of policies will be adopted.

But these adjustments in the policy mix—both appreciation of Asian currencies against the dollar and the use of fiscal policy to offset any contractionary impact on aggregate demand—will be possible only with cooperation among Asian governments and central banks. Policy adjustments that are in the collective interest are less obviously in the individual interest, and there may be reluctance on the part of countries to take the requisite steps unless they are confident that their neighbors will go along. Thus the looming problem of global imbalances provides yet another reason for creating institutions for strengthening mutual surveillance and facilitating collective policy adjustments in the region. In this sense it provides yet additional impetus for East Asian countries to take another step down the long and winding road ultimately leading to deeper regional integration.

References

Aizenman, Joshua, and Jaewoo Lee. 2005. "International Reserves: Precautionary versus Mercantilist Views, Theory and Evidence." Working Paper 11366. Cambridge, Mass.: National Bureau of Economic Research (May).

Blanchard, Olivier, Francesco Giavazzi, and Filipa Sa. 2005. "The U.S. Current Account and the Dollar." Working Paper 11137. Cambridge, Mass.: National Bureau of Economic Research (February).

Caballero, Ricardo, Emmanuel Fahri, and Pierre-Olivier Gourinchas. 2006. "An Equilibrium Model of 'Global Imbalances' and Low Interest Rates." Working Paper 11996. Cambridge, Mass.: National Bureau of Economic Research (February).

Chang, W. W., and F. Chen. 1994. "Vertically Integrated Markets: Export Rivalry between DC and LDC Firms." *Review of International Economics* 2: 131–42.

Edwards, Sebastian. 2005. "Is the U.S. Current Account Deficit Sustainable? And If Not, How Costly Is Adjustment Likely to Be?" NBER Working Paper 11541. Cambridge, Mass.: National Bureau of Economic Research (August).

Gaulier, Guillaume, Francoise Lemoine, and Deniz Unal-Kesencis. 2004. "China's Integration in Asian Production Networks and Its Implications." Tokyo: Research Institute of Economy, Trade and Industry (June 17).

Gourinchas, Pierre-Olivier, and Helene Rey. 2005. "From World Banker to World Venture Capitalist: U.S. External Adjustment and the Exorbitant Privilege." Working Paper 11563. Cambridge, Mass.: National Bureau of Economic Research (August).

Gruber, Joseph W., and Steven Kamin. 2005. "Explaining the Global Pattern of Current Account Imbalances." International Finance Discussion Paper 846. Board of Governors of the Federal Reserve System (November).

Hausmann, Ricardo, and Federico Sturzenegger. 2005. "U.S. and Global Imbalances: Can Dark Matter Prevent a Big Bang?" Kennedy School of Government, Harvard University.

International Monetary Fund (IMF). 2005. "Global Imbalances: A Saving and Investment Perspective." *World Economic Outlook* (May): 91–124.

Kawai, Masahiro, and Taizo Motonishi. 2004. "Is East Asia an Optimum Currency Area?" In *Financial Interdependence and Exchange Rate Regimes in East Asia,* edited by Masahiro Kawai, pp. 157–203. Tokyo: Policy Research Institute, Ministry of Finance.

Kitchen, John. 2006. "Sharecroppers or Shrewd Capitalists? Projections of the U.S. Current Account, International Income Flows, and Net International Debt." U.S. Office of Management and Budget (February).

Lambertini, Luca. 2004. "Intra-Industry Trade under Vertical Product Differentiation." Working Paper 786. Bologna, Italy: Department of Economics, University of Bologna (July).

Mussa, Michael. 2004. "Exchange Rate Adjustments Needed to Reduce Global Payments Imbalances." In *Dollar Adjustment: How Far? Against What?* edited by C. Fred Bergsten and John Williamson, pp. 113–38. Washington: Institute for International Economics.

Obstfeld, Maurice, and Kenneth Rogoff. 2004. "The Unsustainable U.S. Current Account Position Revisited." NBER Working Paper 10869. Cambridge, Mass.: National Bureau of Economic Research (October).

Roubini, Nouriel, and Brad Setser. 2004. "The U.S. as a Net Debtor: The Sustainability of the U.S. External Imbalances." New York University, Stern School of Business (November).

Yoshitomi, Masaru. 2004. "Capital Flows, Exchange Rate Regimes, and Emerging Market Economies in Asia." Speech delivered to the Fiscal Policy Research Institute, Ministry of Finance, Bangkok, January 4.

3

YONGDING YU

Toward East Asian Monetary and Financial Cooperation: A Chinese Perspective

THE ASIAN CRISIS of 1997–98 was no simple matter. Ten years after the fact, the consensus view is that it reflected a combination of domestic and international factors.[1] Domestically, the long-standing practice by governments of enlisting the banking system as an instrument of their industrial policies created vulnerabilities on bank balance sheets. Banks that regarded themselves as too big and politically well connected to fail levered up their bets, creating contingent liabilities for the public sector. Weaknesses in corporate governance allowed firms to borrow excessively, while the maintenance of pegged exchange rates encouraged them to leave their liabilities unhedged. Capital account liberalization was poorly sequenced: it preceded financial strengthening, corporate governance reform, and greater exchange rate flexibility rather than following them, and the access of banks to offshore funding was often liberalized before foreigners were permitted access to bond markets and restrictions on foreign direct investment (FDI) in sensitive sectors were lifted.

International markets, for their part, lent liberally in the first half of the 1990s, financing and thereby encouraging many of these excesses. Then, when confidence was disturbed in the summer of 1997, the direction of capital flows turned on a dime. Assistance from the International Monetary Fund (IMF)

1. The first and still definitive analysis of the event is Goldstein (1998). A representative summary of the subsequent consensus is Sharma (2003).

was slow in coming, and when it came there were onerous conditions attached. The Fund emphasized the domestic roots of the crisis and in so doing contributed to the erosion of confidence. Tellingly, in Asia this episode is frequently referred to as "the IMF crisis" rather than the "Asian financial crisis."

One way of understanding recent interest in monetary cooperation in East Asia is as a response to this last set of observations. East Asian governments concluded that they could not rely on the IMF for assistance when their exchange rates came under attack, since the Fund's assistance came too late or not at all. The experience of the crisis also impressed on Asian governments that they had a better chance of surviving financial market shocks if they pooled their resources instead of attempting to face down market forces individually.

In the years since the crisis, the global and regional financial environment has continued to evolve. Japan's influence in East Asia has eroded as a result of seven additional years of deflation and stagnation, while China's rapid economic growth has heightened that country's influence over the policies of its neighbors. The global financial landscape is now dominated by the twin deficits of the United States, which are leading East Asian countries to accumulate dollar-denominated foreign exchange reserves. Trade frictions are mounting. East Asian countries in general and China in particular are being pressed to revalue their currencies. It is widely argued that resolving the problem of global imbalances may require the dollar to fall against other currencies by an additional 30 percent.[2] The consequences will not be happy for East Asian countries with extensive dollar-denominated foreign exchange reserves that depend on the U.S. market for foreign sales.

This chapter asks how the East Asian countries should respond to these challenges. It focuses on the role of China, in particular. The second and third sections summarize progress to date in strengthening Asia's financial architecture and fostering monetary and financial cooperation. The fourth section identifies the economic and political obstacles to faster progress. The fifth section describes China's transformation and the challenges the country will face in sustaining its rapid growth; it inquires into the implications of the country's emergence for economic and financial cooperation in East Asia. Informed by this analysis, the sixth section sketches some scenarios for the future. The seventh and final section offers some conclusions.

2. A variety of models point to this same conclusion. See for example Blanchard, Giavazzi, and Sa (2005); Obstfeld and Rogoff (2005); Caballero, Farhi, and Gourinchas (2005); and Yoshitomi (chapter 2 in this volume).

The Emerging East Asian Financial Architecture

The first post-crisis initiative by an East Asian government addressing the need for regional monetary and financial cooperation was Japan's proposal in September 1997 to create an Asian Monetary Fund (or AMF). Its objectives were to encourage policy dialogue and regularize emergency financial support, which the IMF had failed to provide in a timely manner and subject to acceptable conditions when needed most.[3] The AMF was intended as a mechanism for disbursing aid faster, subject to conditions that were less demanding and more consonant with the "Asian way." While the demise of the proposal resulted from objections by the United States and the IMF itself to a regional arrangement that might undermine multilateral conditionality, it also reflected the limitations of communication and trust among East Asian countries, especially between China and Japan.

The next significant response was the Chiang Mai Initiative (CMI) announced by the finance ministers of ASEAN, China, Japan, and South Korea (ASEAN+3) in May 2000. The participating governments committed to strengthening policy dialogue and cooperation in areas related to the monitoring of capital flows, the reform of domestic financial arrangements, and the development of a more robust regional financial architecture. At the center of the CMI is the expanded ASEAN Swap Arrangement, itself a network of bilateral swap agreements (or BSAs). Member countries are authorized to borrow liquidity collateralized by domestic currencies and subject to government guarantees. These credit lines are effectively a mechanism enabling the participating countries to pool a portion of their foreign exchange reserves and thus to better fend off pressures from international financial markets. The availability of these swap lines and credits should in turn attenuate the need for individual countries to accumulate large reserve balances as a means of self-insurance.

This network of bilateral swap agreements is sometimes seen as a first step toward the creation of a self-standing set of East Asian financial institutions and arrangements. In this view, out of the Chiang Mai Initiative and the associated BSAs will eventually evolve a regional lender of last resort and, ultimately, a regional central bank. Realism requires observing that these outcomes are a long way off. Only 15 percent of the bilateral credits arranged under the Chiang Mai Initiative can be provided automatically upon request.[4] The remaining 85 percent will be made available only when the borrowing

3. For discussion, see Shinohara (1999).

4. The original figure was 10 percent, which was modestly increased.

country successfully negotiates an IMF program and is therefore subject to IMF conditionality.[5] Thus the possibility that the CMI might evolve into an autonomous regional financial institution has been reduced by self-imposed constraints, reflecting both outside pressures (continued skepticism on the part of the United States and the IMF about the efficacy of this regional arrangement) and doubts within Asian countries about the adequacy of regional surveillance. Significant progress in transforming the CMI into something resembling an Asian Monetary Fund will require eliminating the linkage with IMF conditionality, which is in turn contingent on a higher level of trust and self-confidence in the region. It will require more forceful and forthright regional surveillance to assure the countries extending credits that they will be paid back—that their partners will not draw excessively or make reckless use of the financial resources obtained by activating their BSAs.

Moreover, the goals to which the CMI might ultimately be put—will it be used to support a regional system of exchange rate pegs, for example—were purposely kept vague. This posture of constructive ambiguity was adopted to deflect the kind of criticism that had been directed at Japan's earlier proposal for an Asian Monetary Fund. But this stance has costs, since governments are unlikely to invest significant resources in an arrangement unless its objectives and hence its prospective benefits are clear.[6] In practice, doubts that the BSAs might be activated quickly and automatically and uncertainty about the uses to which they would be put have certainly not discouraged Asian countries from continuing to accumulate international reserves. And as reserve holdings continue to mount, the urgency of expanding regional swap arrangements, making them multilateral, and making their administration autonomous from outside entities diminishes accordingly.

The next step in the development of a regional financial architecture was the Asian Bond Market Initiative (ABMI) in 2003. This initiative reflects the perception that a fundamental cause of the East Asian currency crisis had been excessive reliance on the banking sector as a source of investment finance, coupled with the double-mismatch problem (the existence of pervasive currency and maturity mismatches on national balance sheets, which heightened financial fragility). The ABMI is designed to foster the development of an alternative: a pan-Asian market in long-term debt securities denominated in local currencies. Bringing together investors and issuers in a pan-Asian market promises economies of scale, lower spreads, and greater efficiency. A set of

5. As initially negotiated, the CMI would have also allowed this remaining 90 percent to be drawn if the borrowing country had negotiated a Contingent Credit Line (CCL) with the IMF, but the CCL facility was allowed to expire.

6. See Eichengreen (2003).

regional working groups was established under the umbrella of the ABMI, and numerous conferences and seminars have been convened. The results have included some progress in building the relevant bond market infrastructure and some experimental issuance of local currency bonds, notably by the Asian Development Bank. Optimists like Kuroda (2004) predict that within a relatively short time—say three to five years—the essential prerequisites for regional bond markets can be put in place.

A related initiative by the Executives' Meeting of East Asia-Pacific Central Banks (EMEAP) was the creation of the Asian Bond Fund (ABF).[7] The ABF is designed to catalyze the growth of Asian bond markets by allocating a portion of the reserves of regional central banks to purchases of government and quasi-government securities. The initial U.S.$1 billion of investments, known as ABF1, was devoted to Asian sovereign and quasi-sovereign dollar-denominated bonds. ABF2 is twice as large and includes bonds denominated in regional currencies. It has two components: a U.S.$1 billion central bank reserve pool to be overseen by professional managers for local bond allocation, and a U.S.$1 billion index unit intended to list on eight stock exchanges, beginning with Hong Kong in 2005. The latter is designed to facilitate one-stop entry for retail and institutional buyers and to provide a benchmark structure for tracking pan-Asian performance.[8]

To date, concrete results from these initiatives have been limited. Issuance on Asian bond markets has risen only modestly. Turnover rates and market liquidity remain low by international standards. There is no lack of initiatives to develop Asian financial markets, but there is still a lack of progress.

These, then, are the regional initiatives in the areas of money and finance providing the backdrop to ongoing discussions of the desirability of coordinating exchange rate management in East Asia.

Cooperation on Exchange Rates

Before the Asian financial crisis, East Asian currencies were effectively pegged to the dollar.[9] This link provided an anchor for domestic price levels. It also

7. The members of EMEAP are the Bank of Japan, Bank of Korea, Bank Indonesia, Bank of Thailand, Central Bank of the Philippines, Hong Kong Monetary Authority, Malaysian State Bank, Monetary Authority of Singapore, People's Bank of China, Reserve Bank of Australia, and Reserve Bank of New Zealand.

8. In a related proposal, Ito (2004) has suggested that Asian basket currency government bonds (ABC government bonds) could be created to help diversify currency risk and reduce reliance on bank loans.

9. McKinnon (2000) has dubbed this arrangement the East Asian dollar standard.

stabilized intraregional exchange rates, since the various East Asian currencies were all pegged to the same external numeraire.

There is less agreement on how to characterize post-crisis exchange rate regimes. Some argue that the majority of East Asian countries have moved to regimes of greater flexibility. Others insist that central banks and governments have really restored their de facto dollar pegs, although these are now cloaked in assertions that the authorities have been converted to the merits of greater flexibility.[10]

To be sure, pegging to the dollar has weaknesses. Since the Plaza Accord of 1985, economic growth in Asia has tended to accelerate whenever the yen appreciates and decelerate whenever the yen depreciates.[11] Thus pegging to the yen rather than the dollar—or, more plausibly, in addition to the dollar—could buttress macroeconomic stability and moderate the severity of macroeconomic cycles. Since emerging Asian countries export to both the United States and Japan, their effective exchange rates would be more stable.[12] Imported demand disturbances would also be less pronounced.

Typically, this argument enjoys political support in periods when the yen depreciates and East Asia finds it more difficult to maintain its growth momentum. Conversely, in periods such as 2002–04, when the yen appreciated against the dollar, East Asia enjoyed an accelerating recovery, and shifting to a basket peg came to be seen as less urgent. The consensus view that dollar depreciation is likely to continue as a result of America's twin deficits suggests that there will be continued difficulties in marshaling political support for this case.

If the idea of basket pegs is accepted, the next step will be to reach agreement throughout the region on common basket weights. The idea of a common basket peg has been advanced by a number of authors, most notably John Williamson. In Williamson's view, it would be particularly advantageous for East Asian countries to all adopt the same basket. "This would guarantee . . . that no change in third-country exchange rates could disturb the trading relationships among the East Asian countries themselves," he argues.[13] Other advantages include the creation of a favorable environment for further advances toward regional monetary integration, should this goal be viewed as desirable.

But there are also problems with a common basket. East Asian economies differ in their economic structures, their trading partners, and their policy objectives. This is evident when one contemplates proposals that they all

10. For more evidence on this, see chapter 5 by Kawai in this volume.

11. See Kwan (2001).

12. As documented by Yoshino, Kaji, and Suzuki (2005).

13. Williamson (2005, p. 10).

revalue by the same amount to help alleviate the problem of global imbalances. Revaluing by the same amount would have different impacts on different regional economies.[14] Indicative of this fact, different countries have in fact allowed their currencies to adjust against the dollar by different amounts in the first half of the current decade. Some East Asian countries allowed their currencies to appreciate by 25 percent or more between 2002 and 2005. Other countries have sought to more strictly limit the movement of their currencies.[15] Thus at the time of writing, China has limited the appreciation of the renminbi relative to the dollar to a few percentage points, while Hong Kong has prevented its exchange rate against the dollar from moving at all. In addition, as John Williamson argues, a basket numeraire "would leave traders in the participating countries without a mechanism for ascertaining the local currency value of trade contracts that will mature only in the future. An important advantage of a traditional peg to one of the main international currencies, like the dollar, is that traders can expect that a contract denominated in that currency will normally have an unchanged value in terms of the local currency when the contract expires."[16]

These dilemmas are heightened by China's decision to revalue by 2.1 percent against the dollar on July 21, 2005, and to officially shift to a basket peg. If nothing else, the fact that the renminbi is likely to move more independently of the dollar points up the importance of resolving the ongoing debate about the costs and benefits of a basket peg.

Why Has Progress Been So Slow?

Why then has progress on regional monetary and financial cooperation been so slow? The economist's answer is that East Asia is still far from satisfying the conditions for an optimum currency area.[17] Different countries are at different stages of development. Their economic structures are very different. China is still heavily agricultural, and rural residents still account for 60 percent of total population. Japan, in contrast, is highly industrialized. A realistic forecast is

14. McKibbin and Stoeckel (2003) present a simulation analysis of the effects. See also the discussion by Yoshitomi in chapter 2 of this volume.

15. These limited movements have only fanned expectations of further appreciation, which have in turn attracted further speculative capital into Asian financial markets, aggravating the difficulty of sterilization and forcing additional accumulation of foreign reserves. See Genberg, McCauley, Park, and Persaud (2005).

16. Williamson (2005, p.12).

17. The classic references here, of course, are Mundell (1961), McKinnon (1963), and Kenen (1969).

that it will take China 40 years to catch up with Japan in terms of levels of per capita income; that is to say, these differences in economic structure will persist. The East Asian economies also have pronounced differences in the composition of their exports. More advanced economies such as Japan, Singapore, South Korea, and Taiwan export knowledge- and capital-intensive products, while others such as China and Vietnam specialize in relatively labor-intensive goods and will likely continue to do so for some time.

An implication is that business cycles in the region are far from synchronized. While Japan has been bogged down in recession since the early 1990s, China has experienced rapid growth. Where Japan has been suffering from deflation, China has alternated between inflation and price stability. Economic conditions in other countries are similarly heterogeneous. East Asian countries experiencing different macroeconomic conditions naturally prefer different macroeconomic policies. This poses an obvious obstacle for those who would like to encourage governments and central banks to harmonize their policies, adopt a common currency peg, or even more ambitiously, start planning for a single currency.

In addition, the policy instruments available for managing external shocks differ across countries. In China capital controls and tight financial regulation were key instruments for containing market volatility during the Asian financial crisis, and even now, the Chinese authorities rely more on market guidance than market-based instruments (interest rates) when seeking to influence the rate of growth of bank lending. In Hong Kong, which has more advanced financial markets, the key policy instrument was and is the inter-bank interest rate. National economies are likely to respond differently even to symmetric shocks since they have different adjustment mechanisms and policies at their command.[18] This is yet another problem for those wishing to argue that Asian countries should stabilize their exchange rates against one another by harmonizing their monetary policies.

Finally, labor mobility—the alternative adjustment mechanism identified by the theory of optimum currency areas—is underdeveloped in Asia. Japan's aversion to immigration is well known, and the record of the other East Asian countries is not much better. There are some prominent exceptions (Philippine guest workers in Hong Kong, for example), but the development of labor mobility has considerably further to go before East Asia begins to satisfy this criterion.

In sum, there is still an urgent need to deploy country-specific monetary and fiscal policies. An external constraint that requires national policies to be

18. Bayoumi and Eichengreen (1993) show how the empirical literature on optimum currency areas can be extended from asymmetric shocks to asymmetric adjustment mechanisms.

strictly harmonized across countries would be costly for the foreseeable future, and it would be perceived as such.

In other respects, East Asian countries better satisfy the criteria for an optimum currency area. Levels of intraregional trade are comparable to those of Europe when that continent initiated its transition to monetary union.[19] This is especially true for the three key Northeast Asian countries, China, Japan, and South Korea, which are one another's most important or second most important trading partners.

In addition, the elaboration of East Asian supply chains continues to link yet additional countries into this regional network: first Vietnam, now Laos and others. Before the 1990s, the regional division of labor was commonly characterized by the so-called "flying geese" pattern, in which late-developing economies took on the structural characteristics of their earlier-developing counterparts, and these similarities in structure limited the scope for intraregional trade. But with the collapse of the flying geese formation in the 1990s and with impetus from the multinational corporations that became increasingly prominent in the region, a new regional division of labor took shape based on supply chains and a vertical differentiation—one that provides increased scope for intraregional trade. The high-income countries of East Asia produce capital goods, which they export to the middle-income countries of the region. The middle-income countries use these capital goods, in turn, in their production of consumer goods for export. The high-income countries also produce parts and components that are assembled in China and the lower-income East Asian countries for export to the United States and elsewhere.

Trade liberalization and technological change (particularly the revolution in information and communications technologies) have reinforced these trends. They have prompted changes in corporate organization and strategy and encouraged a growing range of activities to be outsourced to enterprises in neighboring countries. Trade in parts and components is growing. Processing trade is flourishing. This new trade pattern has the effect of consolidating the close economic ties among the East Asian economies. As a result of these new trade and investment linkages, the correlation of business cycles in the region is rising, making coordinated policy actions more attractive.

But even if Asia does not yet meet the conditions for an optimum currency area, one should recall that neither did Europe when it undertook the transition to monetary union. Europe still possesses neither labor mobility nor wage

19. Admittedly, the comparison is complicated by the fact that intraregional trade is even more heavily composed of parts and components (more of it takes the form of vertical intra-industry trade) in the Asian than the European case. See the discussion that follows.

flexibility comparable to those of the United States.[20] That this now may be starting to change is a reminder that the optimum currency area criteria are endogenous to a considerable degree.[21] Ultimately, the implications of the theory of optimum currency areas are ambiguous, as always.

Other motives for regional financial cooperation are not as easily understood in terms of the theory of optimum currency areas. For example, establishing a regional rescue mechanism or emergency credit line is easier when it involves pooling together the reserves of countries with very different characteristics and structures that are likely to be subjected to shocks and in need of assistance at different times. From the point of view of this argument, East Asia's economic heterogeneity is an advantage.

The real issue is whether countries can develop the solidarity and political will to limit their own sovereign prerogatives in the interest of economic and financial integration. When during the Asian crisis Eisuke Sakakibara, then Japan's vice minister of finance for international affairs, proposed creating an AMF, his ideas were met with a tepid response within the region, for the reasons noted above, and were criticized by countries and institutions outside the region, as well.

With hindsight, the failure of the AMF exposed a lack of trust and absence of common purpose among Asian countries. It was a reflection of East Asian countries' lack of clear vision on how to preserve peace and prosperity. Here Japan and China hold the key to the future of regional financial cooperation. If China's rise causes a sense of insecurity in Japan and creates desires there to contain the rising power, Tokyo may respond by attempting to further deepen its special relationship with the United States. Progress in Asian monetary and financial cooperation will require Japan to resist the temptation of responding in this way. China, for its part, will have to share its growing power, and not just with Japan, if it wishes to foster the development of an East Asian Economic Community.

Growth and Structural Change in China

Already China's economic power is too considerable for its role in regional monetary and financial affairs to be ignored. If the country continues growing at anything approaching the current pace, its economic power and hence its role in efforts to build regional monetary and financial institutions will become even more substantial.

20. Some documentation of this point is provided by Kiss (2000).

21. That the growth of regional supply chains and vertically integrated intra-industry trade are increasing the correlation of national business cycles, as described in the preceding paragraph, is another instance of the same phenomenon.

To place these issues in perspective, it is useful to start by considering China's economic rise in more detail. Over the past 25 years, China has maintained an annual average growth rate of more than 9 percent (see figure 3-1). In 1990 China's GDP was U.S.$388 billion, which accounted for 1.7 percent of the world total and ranked the country as ninth in terms of size. In 2003 its GDP reached U.S.$1.4 trillion, which accounted for 3.9 percent of the world total and placed the country seventh in the world. In 2004 its GDP surpassed U.S.$1.65 trillion at current exchange rates, making China the world's sixth largest economy. China's near-double-digit growth in 2005 and revisions of the official statistics, which further raised Chinese GDP (by some 15 percent), have now vaulted the country into fifth place in the growth leagues (again using market exchange rates for purposes of comparison).[22] China's trade surplus will exceed U.S.$70 billion in 2005, and its foreign exchange reserves will soon exceed U.S.$1 trillion.

Internal pressure to maintain these rapid growth rates is considerable. It will be necessary for China to find jobs in the modern sector for workers rendered redundant by the restructuring of state enterprises and for rural residents seeking to find employment in modern manufacturing, where they will enjoy higher wages and more regular work. It is estimated that 15 million rural workers will relocate in urban areas in every year of the coming decade. A further 5 million workers rendered redundant by the restructuring of state enterprises and for other reasons will similarly have to find jobs in the modern manufacturing sector annually. Thus in order to prevent unemployment and underemployment from rising, the country will have to create at least 20 million jobs each year.

In the past, the elasticity of employment with respect to economic growth was on the order of 0.8. But a number of observers now argue that this elasticity has fallen, perhaps to as little as 0.2.[23] Rising wages have encouraged more capital-intensive production, and high savings and investment rates have made such changes in factor proportions possible. Given the growth of labor productivity, reflecting both this rise in capital intensity and the associated technical change, the country must maintain a very high growth rate of GDP to create the requisite number of jobs. This explains China's insistence on the maintenance of an

22. If one values GNP at purchasing power parity, China vaults into second place in the global GNP ranking. In per capita terms, China's achievement is also impressive. In 1990 China's per capita GDP was only U.S.$339. By 2003 it had more than tripled, surpassing U.S.$1,000. China may double its GDP per capita from 2000 to 2010. In 2004 China became the third largest trading nation in the world, with total trade surpassing U.S.$1.2 trillion.

23. This was the view of Bai Heijin, then director general of the Economic Research Institute of the State Planning Development Commission, quoted by *People's Daily* Online ("Official Expatiates on China's Macro Control-Regulation Goals," www.peoplesdaily.com [November 20, 2002]).

Figure 3-1. *China's GDP Growth and Inflation, 1976–2004*

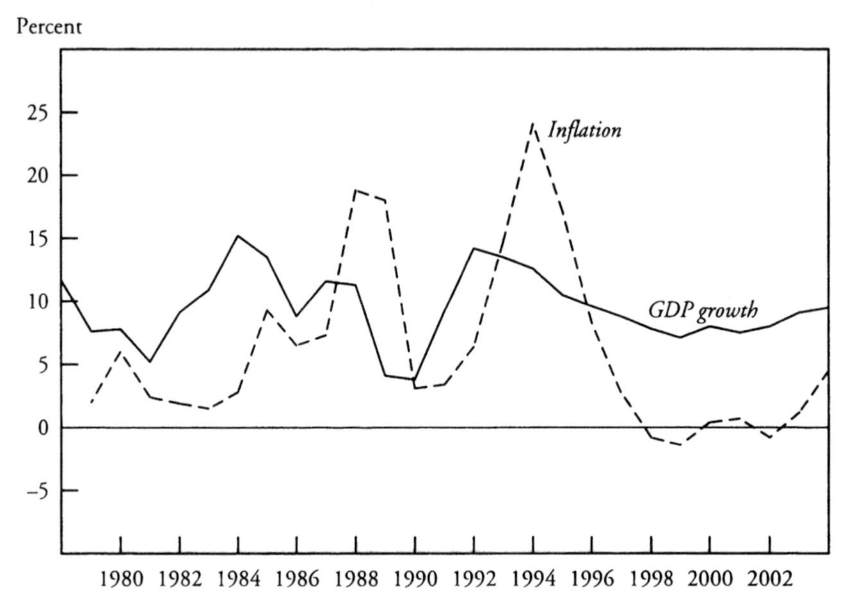

Source: Fang (2005).

exchange rate that is stable and competitively valued against the dollar; these exchange rate policies promise to boost the growth of the export sector and make inward foreign direct investment (FDI) more attractive, in the view of Michael Dooley, David Folkerts-Landau, and Peter Garber.[24]

While Dooley, Folkerts-Landau, and Garber's thesis has come in for considerable critical analysis, the authors are basically right in observing that it is the authorities' emphasis on job creation that keeps them wedded to the traditional strategy of export- and FDI-led growth. China has a large export sector, including a number of highly labor-intensive industries. In 2003 more than 18 million workers were in textiles and apparel alone, making these industries the largest employers in the country. Fear that even a small revaluation of the renminbi would lead to the loss of millions of textile and apparel jobs was an important factor in the authorities' reluctance to see the currency rise.

But the strategy of export- and FDI-led growth based on a highly competitive exchange rate also has costs. The rapid growth of Chinese exports fans protectionist sentiment in other countries, not least the United States, and may have adverse implications for global financial stability insofar as it allows

24. See Dooley, Folkerts-Landau, and Garber (2003).

the United States to avoid coming to terms with its twin deficits. It encourages overinvestment in manufacturing while depressing capital formation in the service sector. And, arguably, the balance of benefits and costs is changing over time, with the costs becoming ever more apparent.

All this raises questions about the sustainability of China's existing growth model and raises the possibility that adjustments are in the offing.

First, China will have to rely more on domestic demand relative to external demand. Its trade-to-GDP ratio was over 70 percent and rising at the end of 2004 (where trade is defined as the sum of exports and imports). This dependence on foreign demand heightens the economy's vulnerability to external shocks and exposes the country to cyclical movements in the world economy. China's export drive has provoked worries abroad and fanned protectionist sentiment. Technological imperatives will also make it more difficult to maintain the country's export drive. Expanding the range of Chinese exports will require producers to move into more knowledge- and technology-intensive products, and their capacity to do so will be predicated on the development of an economy based more on innovation, which will take time to emerge. For these and other reasons, the economy may be about to run up against limits on the ability of its export sector to continue growing at its current pace. Reduced dependence on foreign markets for demand and on the export sector for job creation imply that the authorities may grow more sympathetic to an exchange rate that is allowed to fluctuate more freely in general and against the dollar in particular.

Second, enhancing the role of domestic demand will involve encouraging household spending. To accomplish this, the government must improve the social security system, the delivery of health care, and the provision of education so that the incentive for precautionary savings on the part of households can be reduced. Structural change in the public sector—the creation of modern pension, health care, and education systems—is fundamental to this transformation. In this context, allowing the renminbi to strengthen is another way of boosting the purchasing power of Chinese households.

Third, China needs to focus more on the quality rather than simply the quantity of investment.[25] By most measures the efficiency of investment has been declining. An important step in the direction of correcting this will be reform of the financial system, so that the provision of external finance is limited to firms with high-return investment projects. In addition, fears that appreciation of the currency will hurt profitability and depress investment in

25. This is fundamental to the transition from the old system of central planning to a market economy, insofar as the planners focused on quantitative targets for capital formation (and the old planning system was notorious for overinvestment).

marginal sectors may influence policy less powerfully in the future than the past. Raising the quality of investment will require allowing investment in low-return sectors to tail off. If China is to achieve this, then a strengthening of the currency that causes investment to be more heavily concentrated in the most profitable and competitive sectors will not be a bad thing.

Fourth, Chinese growth will become less FDI-intensive. In turn this will have implications for the balance of payments and the exchange rate. Normally, the surplus derived from FDI on the capital account and the deficit caused by imports of capital goods on the current account cancel out one other. However, many Chinese enterprises attracting FDI do not directly use the foreign currency provided by international investors to purchase equipment and machinery abroad. Rather they convert the foreign funds into RMB credits, which they use to purchase additional inputs into production on domestic markets. The ample availability of these funds can be seen as another mechanism encouraging too much low-quality investment. Hence to improve resource allocation in general and the quality of investment in particular, policies favoring FDI should be phased out. If China does in fact eventually move away from its FDI-led growth strategy, this will eliminate or at least weaken the authorities' traditional preference for keeping the renminbi stable and competitively valued against the dollar.

Fifth, since China is a high-growth economy, its real effective exchange rate will have to appreciate, consistent with the Balassa-Samuelson effect, in order to shift additional resources into the service sector. This can occur in two ways: through an appreciation of the nominal rate or accelerating domestic inflation. The first alternative would clearly be better from the point of view of monetary policy credibility.

From all this, it is clear that China will have to move toward a more diversified, less export- and FDI-centered development model in coming years. In turn this will have implications for its exchange rate policy and, more broadly, for regional monetary and financial cooperation.

Implications of China's Development for Regional Cooperation

One possibility is that China's increasing reliance on domestic demand and reduced dependence on foreign markets will diminish its interest in economic, financial, and monetary cooperation with its neighbors. As China comes to direct the majority of its production to the domestic market, arguments about the need for regional monetary and exchange rate cooperation to help stabilize its terms of access to external markets will lose some of their urgency.

To be sure, China will remain an export-oriented economy in the near future, and as such it will continue to be interested in exchange rate stability. But between this interest and the creation of a single Asian currency remains a considerable gulf. When it comes to policy reform, the Chinese authorities are known for their preference for gradualism (for "crossing the river by feeling the stones," in the words of Deng Xiaoping). In the current context, gradualism means that they are likely to prefer a series of small steps in the direction of greater monetary cooperation. At each step they will wait and evaluate the benefits before proceeding. This preference for gradualism implies that the further elaboration of monetary cooperation in the region is likely to be a drawn-out process.

Moreover, it is hard to imagine that China will be on the receiving end of a financial rescue package for the foreseeable future, notwithstanding the existence of serious problems in its banking system. China has extensive financial reserves, some of which have already been used to recapitalize the banking system. And even if a bailout is required, the country is simply too large for its Asian neighbors to underwrite it. The Chinese government is therefore likely to be less interested than neighboring Asian governments in the further elaboration of the Chiang Mai Initiative and the eventual creation of an Asian Monetary Fund. Moreover, China as a large country is likely to have a greater voice in the deliberations of the IMF and thus to be less interested in pursuing regional alternatives.

The likely result is that China will participate in discussions of East Asian financial cooperation but that it will not take the lead. It will be more active in promoting East Asian free trade agreements (FTAs) than East Asian financial cooperation insofar as its dependence on foreign trade is greater than its dependence on foreign finance. While it may contribute to the expansion of the Chiang Mai Initiative, it is unlikely to support the evolution of the CMI into an Asian Monetary Fund. Since the Chinese authorities attach priority to the further development of domestic financial markets, which promise to enhance the efficiency of investment and facilitate the adoption of a more flexible exchange rate, the country will remain a supporter of the Asian Bond Market Initiative and the Asian Bond Fund. However, reflecting the relatively underdeveloped state of China's bond markets, especially its corporate bond markets, it is likely to remain on the periphery of the ABMI and ABF for the time being.

In conjunction with its 2.1 percent revaluation against the dollar in July 2005, China adopted as the reference point for its exchange rate policy a basket that includes a number of Asian currencies. It is tempting to see this as signaling the country's interest in the pursuit of more closely coordinated East Asian exchange rate policies. As the renminbi is permitted to fluctuate more freely against the basket, its movement will begin to resemble that of other basket-based currencies, such as the Singapore dollar. In turn this will create scope for the harmonization of policies among the central banks responsible for management of these currencies.

But this is for the future. For now the process of exchange rate reform in China is still in its infancy. It will take time to develop the requisite market infrastructure and for policymakers in Beijing and Shanghai to gain the experience needed to operate a more flexible exchange rate. More time will have to pass before China is ready to cooperate with its neighbors on, say, the adoption of a common basket peg or for a regional currency grid to become possible. Similarly, participation in joint action such as a collective revaluation against the dollar is simply out of question for the time being.

Individual Asian countries have taken some modest steps to diversify their reserves. However, reserve diversification presents a collective-action problem. Individual countries have every incentive to diversify their reserves, but if they do so collectively they can cause the dollar to crash, with decidedly negative implications for their economies. This is an argument for coordinating policies toward reserve diversification in order to avoid a stampede out of dollars. However, discussions of this are still in their infancy. For the time being, the question of how to allocate reserves between dollars, euros, yen, gold, and other assets is regarded as too sensitive a national prerogative to permit explicit coordination within the region.

A Road Map for the Future

A study by the Institute of World Economics and Politics at the Chinese Academy of Social Sciences, with which the author is affiliated, has proposed a road map for strengthening East Asia's financial architecture.[26] First on its list is strengthening the Chiang Mai Initiative by institutionalizing information exchange, regularizing policy reviews, and loosening the linkage with IMF conditionality. Second is promoting the development of a regional bond market. This would involve developing domestic bond markets, especially in the countries where they are still in their infancy, and laying the groundwork for an integrated regional market. The Asian Bond Fund can be seen as the first phase of these efforts, which still have a long way to go.

Once this is accomplished it may be possible to begin thinking about arrangements for fostering a greater degree of intraregional exchange rate stabil-

26. Institute of World Economics and Politics (2004).

ity. These can start with international accords for concerted intervention in foreign exchange markets. It will then be possible to contemplate establishing a common currency basket, a parallel currency, and so forth. The success of these efforts will hinge on the willingness of governments and central banks to achieve closer convergence of economic policies and outcomes.

It goes without saying that these ambitious goals require political commitment. Realism requires acknowledging that, for the time being, the requisite degree of political solidarity and cohesion is not in place. This suggests that governments should focus for now on strengthening their national economies and putting in place the policies, including exchange rate policies, best suited to their domestic economic needs. They should develop their domestic financial markets and regularize the provision of mutual supports. Once these processes are more advanced and political will is stronger, the time will be ripe to reinvigorate the process of regional cooperation.

References

Bayoumi, Tamim, and Barry Eichengreen. 1993. "Shocking Aspects of European Monetary Unification." In *Adjustment and Growth in the European Monetary Union,* edited by Francisco Torres and Francesco Giavazzi, pp.193–240. Cambridge University Press.

Blanchard, Olivier, Francesco Giavazzi, and Filippa Sa. 2005. "International Investors, the U.S. Current Account, and the Dollar." *BPEA*, no. 1: 1–66.

Caballero, Ricardo, Emmanuel Farhi, and Pierre-Olivier Gourinchas. 2005. "An Equilibrium Model of 'Global Imbalances' and Low Interest Rates." MIT and University of California–Berkeley.

Dooley, Michael P., David Folkerts-Landau, and Peter Garber. 2003. "An Essay on the Revived Bretton Woods System." Working Paper 9971. Cambridge, Mass.: National Bureau of Economic Research.

Eichengreen, Barry. 2003. "What to Do with the Chiang Mai Initiative." *Asian Economic Papers* 2: 1–49.

Fang, Cai. 2005. "How to Realize Growth in the Economy and Employment at the Same Time." *Monthly Bulletin of the Chinese Economic Forum of 50 Persons*, 8: 31–49.

Genberg, Hans, Robert McCauley, Yung Chul Park, and Avinash Persaud. 2005. *Official Reserves and Currency Management in Asia: Myth, Reality, and the Future*, Geneva Reports on the World Economy 7. London: Center for Economic Policy Research.

Goldstein, Morris. 1998. *The Asian Financial Crisis.* Washington: Institute for International Economics.

Ito, Takatoshi. 2004. "Promoting Asian Basket Currency Bonds." In *Developing Asian Bond Markets,* edited by Takatoshi Ito and Yung Chul Park. Australian National University, Asia Pacific Press.

Institute of World Economics and Politics. 2004. "East Asian Financial and Exchange Rate Cooperation." Ministry of Finance, People's Republic of China (July).

Kenen, Peter. 1969. "The Theory of Optimum Currency Areas: An Eclectic View." In *Monetary Problems of the International Economy,* edited by Robert Mundell and Alexander Swoboda, pp. 41–60. University of Chicago Press.

Kiss, Elinda Fishman. 2000. "Optimum Currency Areas: The Euro as a Practical Paradigm?" Rutgers University.

Kuroda, Haruhiko. 2004. "Transitional Steps in the Road to a Single Currency in East Asia." Paper presented to the Seminar on a Single Currency for East Asia: Lessons from Europe. Asian Development Bank, Jeju Island, South Korea, May 14.

Kwan, C. H. 2001. *Yen Bloc: Toward Economic Integration in Asia.* Brookings.

McKibbin, Warwick, and Andrew Stoeckel. 2003. "What if China Revalues Its Currency?" *Economic Scenarios* 7 (December).

McKinnon, Ronald I. 1963. "Optimum Currency Areas." *American Economic Review* 53: 717–25.

———. 2000. "After the Crisis, the East Asian Dollar Standard Resurrected: An Interpretation of High-Frequency Exchange Rate Pegging." Stanford University, Department of Economics.

Mundell, Robert. 1961. "The Theory of Optimum Currency Areas." *American Economic Review* 51: 657–65.

Obstfeld, Maurice, and Kenneth Rogoff. 2005. "Global Exchange Rate Adjustments and Global Current Account Balances." *BPEA,* no. 1: 67–123.

Sharma, Shalendra. 2003. *The Asian Financial Crisis.* Manchester University Press.

Shinohara, Hajime. 1999. "On the Asian Monetary Fund." *Institute of International Monetary Affairs Newsletter.* Tokyo: Institute for International Monetary Affairs (March 31).

Williamson, John. 2005. "A Currency Basket for East Asia, Not Just China." Policy Brief 05-1. Washington: Institute for International Economics.

Yoshino, Naoyuki, Sahoko Kaji, and Ayako Suzuki. 2005. "The Basket-Peg, Dollar-Peg, and Floating: A Comparative Analysis." *Journal of the Japanese and International Economies* 19: 183–217.

4

KWANHO SHIN
YUNJONG WANG

The Linkage between Trade Agreements and Monetary Cooperation

Economic integration is high on the policy agenda in East Asia. One way of proceeding would be to focus on intraregional trade and investment and attempt to foster their further expansion through the negotiation of free trade agreements (FTAs) and investment arrangements. Another, conceivably complementary, approach would be to focus on monetary integration and to seek to develop a regional currency arrangement leading ultimately to an East Asian monetary union. It is not obvious which strategy would be most productive.

In a previous article we questioned whether trade integration is a necessary precursor to monetary integration.[1] We argued that trade agreements among East Asian countries might be slow to materialize and could be stymied by domestic political resistance. This suggests that it might be advisable for countries to attempt to leap directly to closer monetary integration. Among the advantages of this approach is the possibility that exchange rate stabilization leading to deeper monetary integration might lend further stimulus to intraregional trade and that this might in turn render regional free trade agreements more attractive.

Our observation finds some support in subsequent developments, in the sense that the prospects for a regionwide FTA encompassing the ASEAN+3 countries (the 10 members of ASEAN plus China, Japan, and South Korea)

1. See Shin and Wang (2004).

remain remote. The two largest East Asian economies, China and Japan, continue to exhibit a preference for bilateral arrangements. Geopolitical rivalry between the two countries and their unsettled historical legacy further cloud the picture. All this raises the danger that if trade integration is viewed as a precondition for monetary integration, difficulties in achieving the first objective might prevent Asian countries from achieving the second.

In this chapter, we seek to shed further light on the connections between trade and monetary integration. In doing so we are exploring largely uncharted terrain. Neither theory nor evidence has been effectively mobilized to address the question of whether regional trade arrangements (RTAs) do more to encourage monetary and exchange rate cooperation among the participating countries, or vice versa, and which should come first.[2] In East Asia, in particular, debate on the feasibility and desirability of FTAs has mostly abstracted from the linkage to monetary integration. The implications of the exchange rate regime for the political economy of an East Asia FTA are taken as subsidiary considerations—to the extent that they are discussed at all.

That attention has not yet focused on these issues reflects, in part, the fact that an ASEAN+3 free trade area is still in its formative stages. The current pattern of trade agreements is essentially bilateral; as yet there is no formal ongoing effort to build a regionwide, multilateral agreement like Europe's Common Market. (An exception is the ASEAN Free Trade Area, or AFTA, but as discussed later in this chapter, this has at yet had little discernible positive impact on intraregional trade.) Bilateral agreements of the sort that have dominated East Asian trade negotiations to date are unlikely to foster the kind of cohesive collective policy framework needed to support monetary cooperation at the regional level. Quite apart from the policy framework, monetary cooperation requires a durable political commitment. And, in East Asia, the relevant level of political cohesion simply does not exist.

In Europe, adoption of a trade integration-first strategy was natural, given the importance of intraregional trade for European recovery in the aftermath of World War II. In the wake of the war, other European countries depended on Germany for the provision of capital goods, while Germany depended on its neighbors for consumer goods that were not readily produced at home. Moreover, when the Treaty of Rome was negotiated in 1957, the idea of setting up a regional exchange rate coordination mechanism or of introducing a common currency was less pressing because the Bretton Woods system of pegged but adjustable exchange rates provided adequate levels of exchange rate stability both in Europe and worldwide. Only when the Bretton Woods

2. This observation is further developed in Eichengreen and Taylor (2003).

system began to unravel did pressure develop for regional exchange rate stabilization measures and serious discussions of European monetary integration begin.

The North American Free Trade Agreement (NAFTA), another precedent that might conceivably be followed in Asia, was created without explicit consideration of the need for exchange rate stability. To be sure, when the peso crashed in December 1994, the United States provided financial assistance to Mexico and encouraged the International Monetary Fund (IMF) to do likewise, but this was an ad hoc reaction and not an institutionalized response. It is now taken for granted that NAFTA focuses on the integration of trade and production, while monetary management should be left to the national authorities. The Canadian dollar continues to float against the U.S. dollar, and the Mexican peso has grown more flexible with the passage of time. This is in contrast to the situation in Europe, where it has been possible to address a wider range of issues, including monetary ones, because of a willingness to at least contemplate a confederate governance structure.[3]

In the remainder of this chapter we analyze the linkages between trade and monetary integration in more detail. We show that while intra-East Asian trade as a percentage of East Asia total trade has been rising steadily, this rising trend is entirely attributable to China. We conjecture that the two major obstacles to further progress are the exchange rate volatility experienced since the Asian crisis of 1997–98 and the relatively slow materialization of FTAs involving China, Japan, and South Korea.

Building on these observations, we investigate how exchange rate variability influences trade liberalization—if at all. Using a gravity model we estimate the impact of free trade agreements on intraregional trade and examine whether exchange rate volatility lessens the positive effect of those FTAs. We find some evidence that high exchange rate volatility reduces trade. But despite this direct negative effect of exchange rate volatility on bilateral trade, we also find that the level of exchange rate volatility does not diminish the positive impact of FTAs on trade among the participating countries, at least in the case of East Asia. Interestingly, the negative effect of exchange rate volatility on trade appears to have been larger in Europe. Moreover, in Europe high levels of bilateral exchange rate volatility appear to have hampered the growth of intraregional trade not just through their direct effects but also by attenuating the positive impact of the Common Market. These findings thus may help to explain why European countries have, historically, attached such importance to regional initiatives designed to limit exchange rate variability.

3. See Courchene and Harris (2000).

The results for East Asia are less clear-cut. The gravity model fits the data less well, reflecting the high volume of trade between ASEAN members and their more distant East Asian trading partners, Japan and South Korea. The estimated effect of AFTA membership is now negative. In other words, trade among AFTA members has been growing less rapidly than trade among Asian countries generally—even after controlling for country size, distance, and similar factors. This, clearly, is the China effect: China's trade with its neighbors has been expanding enormously, and limiting the sample to Asian countries places this fact in bold relief. But our key result continues to hold even in this subsample: there is little evidence that exchange rate volatility has a negative effect on the growth of trade and on the trade-creating effects of regional agreements in Asia. Our conclusion remains that the slow progress of regional FTAs has limited the pressure for measures to stabilize exchange rates, while those limited measures that have been taken on the exchange rate front in turn have had little impact in terms of magnifying the positive effects of FTAs.

The rest of the chapter is organized as follows. The second and third sections highlight the contrasting experiences of Europe and the Americas and draw out some implications of this history for East Asia. The fourth section describes the progress of trade integration in East Asia and highlights the obstacles to further progress. The fifth section then analyzes how exchange rate volatility conditions the anticipated trade promotion effects of FTAs. The sixth section, finally, concludes with some speculations about the future.

Lessons from Europe

At its inception, the members of the European Economic Communities or European Community (EC) tended to dismiss monetary cooperation as a regional project. To be sure, the European Payments Union set up in 1950 can be credited for having facilitated the resumption of intra-European trade. But little serious attention was then given to the possibility of creating a regional exchange rate coordination mechanism before the 1970s, the Bretton Woods system providing fully for the stability of European currencies.

In the 1960s the main issue in the monetary area was whether exchange rate changes might disrupt the functioning of the Community's nascent customs union and of its Common Agricultural Policy (CAP). Toward the end of the decade, however, divergences in inflation rates and external balances developed among EC member states. In 1968 a speculative attack on the French franc put pressure on intra-Community exchange rates. Policymakers turned their attention to the need for more systematic coordination of economic and monetary policies and for facilities to provide mutual balance of payments assistance in times of crisis. The Werner Plan tabled in 1970 and endorsed by the Community's Council of Ministers in 1971 took these ideas further by recommending the adoption of a single European currency. However, the Werner Plan was quickly abandoned, perhaps predictably, since the political preconditions for creating a single currency and establishing an institution responsible for managing it, a European Central Bank, were not yet in place.

The main practical outcome was a new system, the Snake, for limiting fluctuations in exchange rates among member countries. (Some candidates for accession to the European Community also participated in the system even while they still belonged to the European Free Trade Area, a rival arrangement that eventually became an anteroom for prospective EC members.) But with the collapse of the Bretton Woods system, national policies diverged further, complicating efforts to stabilize exchange rates. Increasingly, policies were formulated at the national level with little attention to the consequences for Europe as a whole. The United Kingdom was quickly forced by its commitment to expansionary policies and lack of competitiveness to abandon the Snake. A series of other EC governments followed suit (the French twice). The result was a climate of conflict and recrimination in which further progress toward a monetary union was impossible.

By 1977, the then nine members of the European Community had effectively sorted themselves into two groups with very different economic performance characteristics and hence different exchange rate regimes.[4] The first group, consisting of Germany, the Benelux countries, and Denmark, with Norway as an associate (non-EC) member, had some success in moderating inflation and sustaining the operation of the Snake. Members of the second group, consisting of the United Kingdom, France, Italy, and Ireland, were not able to subordinate domestic policies to the imperatives of their regional exchange rate arrangement. They were forced to repeatedly float their currencies while experiencing high inflation, current account deficits, and substantial depreciations. All this made it highly challenging, to say the least, to devise an exchange rate system that might successfully encompass both groups of countries.

The liberalization of intra-European trade also slowed in the 1970s, owing in part to the disruptive effects of this exchange rate volatility (together with those of the global productivity slowdown, the two oil shocks, and the so-called new protectionism). Countries experiencing high wage and price inflation were tempted to depreciate their currencies as a way of regaining their

4. On January 22, 1972, after difficult negotiations, the United Kingdom, along with Denmark, Ireland, and Norway, signed the Treaty of Accession with the European Community. In a subsequent referendum, the Norwegian electorate rejected membership.

competitiveness, policies to which their European partners responded by hiking nontariff barriers to trade, or at least slowing their relaxation. This tit-for-tat approach was not conducive to regional integration.

By the late 1970s these problems had created a political consensus, most prominently among French and German leaders but at some level more broadly, on the importance of devising a scheme for limiting intra-EC exchange rate variability, which by this time was not only an obstacle to further integration but posed an increasingly serious threat to the very survival of the economic institutions that Europe had so far succeeded in creating. The result was the next important milestone in European monetary integration, the European Monetary System (EMS). The EMS, created in 1979, consolidated under one umbrella three existing credit facilities: the very short-term financing facility (VSTF), the short-term monetary support facility (STMS), and the medium-term financial assistance facility (MTFA). The new agreement helped to cultivate cooperation among the participating member countries and increasingly provided the focus for European monetary policy. The German Bundesbank pursued policies of low inflation, and other central banks imported its credibility by importing its monetary policies, this link being a mechanical consequence of the pegged exchange rates of the EMS.[5] To be sure, the operation of the EMS was punctuated by periodic realignments in the first half of the 1980s, although after 1986 there were no more changes in central parities.[6] It seemed that, for Europe, exchange rate variability had become a thing of the past.

Not coincidentally, around this time, in 1988, discussions resumed of the possibility that Europe should contemplate deeper monetary integration. In June the Hannover European Council set up a Committee for the Study of Economic and Monetary Union, presided over by the European Commission president, Jacques Delors. In April 1989, the Delors Committee published its Report on Economic and Monetary Union, proposing a three-stage transition to economic and monetary union (EMU).[7] The Delors Report stressed the need for closer coordination of economic policies, rules on the size and financing of national budget deficits, and a new independent institution to be responsible for the single monetary policy.

Initially, the Delors Report received the same cool reception previously encountered by the Werner Plan. It took an exceptional event, the collapse of

5. On this see Volz (2005).

6. Italy moved from the wide (+/– 6 percent) to the narrow (+/– 2 percent) band in 1990, thereby adjusting its margins, but without changing the central parity.

7. See Committee for the Study of Economic and Monetary Union (1989).

the Berlin Wall on November 9, 1989, to trigger a serious reassessment.[8] The prospect that Germany would grow in territory and population by more than a third rendered measures binding that country more closely into Europe a priority for France. And for Germany signaling that it was prepared to rededicate itself to the European project similarly became a priority, with the French reception to German unification still uncertain.

EMU negotiations were concluded at the European Council in Maastricht, the Netherlands, on December 9–10, 1991. The Maastricht Treaty provided for the introduction of economic and monetary union in three stages: a first stage of closer policy coordination; a second stage of institution building along with the decision on who qualified for participation; and a third stage involving the irrevocable locking of exchange rates and, effectively, the transition to monetary union.[9] The negotiations over the second, transitional stage proved particularly difficult.[10] The treaty ultimately provided for the creation of a European Monetary Institute (EMI), to be established in 1994, as a precursor to the European Central Bank. The EMI played an important role in facilitating and reinforcing the coordination of national monetary policies during the transition. Subsequently, member states also adopted a Stability and Growth Pact clarifying the Maastricht Treaty's provisions for dealing with excessive deficits and provided an institutional framework for its enforcement, in part through strengthened surveillance.

Members of the European Community had already become more open to trade with one another as a result of the creation of their customs union. Intra-EC trade as a percentage of GDP had more than doubled between 1960 and 1985. The Single Market Program agreed to in 1986 and completed in 1992 then reinforced these effects. To avoid jeopardizing this accomplishment, EC countries had good reason to take measures to stabilize their exchange rates vis-à-vis one another.

Ultimately, however, Europe's monetary unification project was politically driven. It was informed by the desire to lessen the continent's monetary dependence on the United States. For much of the postwar period, Germany had passively accepted U.S. monetary initiatives rather than attempting to exercise leadership in the operation and development of the international monetary

8. For further discussion see Wyplosz (2001) and Schweickert (2002).

9. The physical introduction of the single currency would then follow.

10. This is not surprising. No one could object to the closer coordination of policies that was the focus of the first stage, while by the third stage the decision over membership and the delegation of monetary policy to the European Central Bank would be complete. This left the second stage as the focus for controversy.

and financial system. The EMS then provided it with a historic opportunity to assume greater responsibility and control, since its currency, the deutsche mark, was the leading currency in Europe, and its central bank, the Bundesbank, had a reputation for pursuing price stability that no other European central bank could match. France for its part sought to stand shoulder to shoulder with Germany in the first division of world powers. The EMS held out hope that, as a result of greater European cooperation and solidarity, the franc's weakness could be reversed. Franco-German cooperation has been at the heart of the development of the European Community ever since.[11] Related to this were the specific post-1990 Franco-German political dynamics alluded to above. (France saw monetary union as a way of locking a reunified Germany into Europe, while Germany saw it as a way of signaling its continued identity as a country of dedicated Europeans.)

Lessons from Other Regions

Regional integration has developed still differently in North America. Given that exports to the United States were fully 87 percent of Canadian exports in 2000, one would think that Canada would have had a compelling incentive to stabilize its exchange rate vis-à-vis the U.S. dollar. But U.S. incentives were different. U.S. exports to Canada were only 18.5 percent of its total (again circa 2000). This asymmetry clearly complicated (and continues to complicate) bilateral cooperation. The United States is reluctant to share decisionmaking power over its monetary policy with its much smaller neighbor to the north. (The same can be said of its attitude toward its smaller neighbor to the south, Mexico.) For Canada the choice therefore boils down to pegging unilaterally and letting the Federal Reserve System determine its monetary policy, or floating its exchange rate. Thus Canada has opted for the second alternative.[12]

11. And even earlier: this process can be traced back at least to the 1960s. Although de Gaulle's nationalism was popular within the country, the General also appreciated that membership in the Common Market would benefit France economically. However, de Gaulle remained implacably opposed to any increase in the powers of the European Commission or to any other increase in supranationalism. He showed how strongly he felt about this in 1965 by precipitating the most dramatic crisis in the history of the European Community (George 1985). It was German Chancellor Helmut Schmidt and French President Valéry Giscard d'Estaing who reinvigorated the integration process at the end of the 1970s. The joint initiative of Chancellor Helmut Kohl and President François Mitterand resulted in a great leap toward EMU at the beginning of the 1990s. The Franco-German alliance formed the core for the integration process in Europe, as it was the political will of these two countries that motivated further integration. See for example Harrop (2000).

12. Historically, Canadian business has lent only tepid support to the campaign for monetary union because it is used to benefiting from the weakness of the currency. However, this historical circumstance

From the comparison of the EU with NAFTA, two elements can be singled out as influencing whether trade integration should be followed by exchange rate and monetary cooperation. First, intraregional trade shares should be large (see table 4-1). This should be true of large countries as well as small ones (recall the contrast between the United States and Canada). Here the implications for East Asia are mixed. In the case of ASEAN, the share of intraregional trade has not increased significantly since the 1970s. To the contrary, the trade concentration ratio has been falling over time. Nor does it appear that preferences under AFTA have significantly boosted intraregional trade.[13]

Second, exchange rate coordination requires even more sophisticated institutional arrangements than a free trade agreement.[14] To be credible, those institutions must be predicated on a willingness to share power. Ability and willingness to move from trade integration to monetary integration, in other words, is contingent on the existence of political will. In the case of Europe, Germany was committed to the European project for historical reasons and thus willing to share power with its smaller neighbors. In North America, in contrast, there is little interest on the part of the regional hegemon, the United States, in power sharing. More generally, there is little support in the region for political integration and hence little scope for extending NAFTA to encompass exchange rate cooperation, much less monetary unification.[15]

Mercosur (the South American customs union of Argentina, Brazil, Paraguay, Uruguay, and Venezuela) offers even less reassurance for those who would like to see an Asian FTA blossom into a regional monetary agreement. When the Brazilian real was devalued in 1999, the Argentine economy came under intense pressure, causing the government of Argentina to backtrack on

---

can change quickly, due to high commodity prices or chronic U.S. deficits, among other reasons. At some point Canadian business may come to realize that exchange rate depreciation provides only very temporary benefits and lend stronger support to the campaign for monetary union. Grubel (2000). To date, however, there is little evidence that this is the case.

13. A number of factors help to explain this. First, about two-thirds of the tariff lines within ASEAN are at the same Most-Favored Nation (MFN) and Common Effective Preferential Tariff (CEPT) levels. As far as the remaining one-third of tariff lines is concerned, the difference between MFN and CEPT rates is small. Hence, less than 5 percent of intraregional trade is covered by CEPT preferences. Second, many products with strong potential for intraregional trade (agricultural products such as rice and sugar and industrial products like automobiles) are politically sensitive, causing a number of members to delay their liberalization to a later date (WTO 2003). More empirical analysis of this point is provided later in the chapter.

14. Eichengreen and Taylor (2003) explore whether the monetary consequences of existing regional trade arrangements mainly reflect spillovers from trade integration or whether observed outcomes have been mainly about politics. Their results support the latter interpretation, which implies that Europe's experience cannot simply be translated to other regions where the political circumstances are different.

15. For evidence and discussion see Eichengreen and Taylor (2003).

Table 4-1. *Intraregional Export Shares, 1970–2001*
Percent

Region and group	*1970*	*1980*	*1985*	*1990*	*1995*	*2000*	*2001*	*Year in force*
Europe and North America								
CEFTA[a]	. . .	. . .	. . .	. . .	14.6	11.5	12.4	1993
European Union	59.5	60.8	59.2	65.9	62.4	62.1	61.2	1957
NAFTA[b]	36.0	33.6	43.9	41.4	46.2	55.7	54.8	1994
Latin America and the Caribbean								
Andean Group	1.8	3.8	3.2	4.2	12.2	8.8	11.2	1988
CACM[c]	26.0	24.4	14.4	15.4	21.7	13.7	15.0	1961
CARICOM[d]	4.2	5.3	6.3	8.1	12.1	14.6	13.4	1973
MERCOSUR[e]	9.4	11.6	5.5	8.9	20.3	20.7	20.8	1991
Africa								
CEAC (UDEAC)[f]	4.8	1.6	1.9	2.3	2.2	1.2	1.3	1999
COMESA[g]	7.4	5.7	4.4	6.3	6.0	4.8	5.2	1994
ECCAS[h]	9.8	1.4	1.7	1.4	1.5	0.9	1.1	1983[o]
ECOWAS[i]	2.9	9.6	5.1	8.0	9.0	9.6	9.8	1975[o]
SADC[j]	4.2	0.4	1.4	3.1	10.6	11.9	10.9	1992
UEMOA[k]	6.2	9.9	8.7	12.1	10.3	13.0	13.5	2000[o]
Middle East and Asia								
ASEAN/AFTA[l]	22.4	17.4	18.6	19.0	24.6	23.0	22.4	1992
GCC[m]	4.6	3.0	4.9	8.0	6.8	5.0	5.1	1981[o]
SAARC[n]	3.2	4.8	4.5	3.2	4.4	4.3	4.9	1985[o]

Sources: UNCTAD, *Handbook of Statistics 2002*; WTO, *International Trade Statistics 2002*.
a. Central European Free Trade Agreement (Bulgaria, Croatia, Romania).

(*continued*)

its bilateral trade commitments. Then the collapse of Argentine convertibility in 2001 caused the exchange rate between the real and the peso to move sharply in the other direction. The momentum for free trade in the Southern Cone has dissolved as a result of the increasingly complex web of exemptions and exceptions adopted in the wake of these events. One would think that the threat posed by exchange rate volatility to the survival of the free trade agreement would have created irresistible pressure for deeper monetary cooperation, but this has not been the case.

What lessons can be drawn from these experiences for the prospects for monetary integration in East Asia? The implication of European experience is that monetary union in Asia is likely to be a long way off and that it can be reached only via a winding path of progressively deeper cooperation and

Table 4-1. *Intraregional Export Shares, 1970–2001 (continued)*

b. North American Free Trade Agreement (Canada, Mexico, United States).

c. Central American Common Market (Costa Rica, El Salvador, Guatemala, Honduras, Nicaragua).

d. Caribbean Common Market (Antigua and Barbuda, Bahamas, Barbados, Belize, Dominica, Guyana, Haiti, Jamaica, Monserrat, Trinidad and Tobago, St. Nevis, St. Lucia, St. Vincent and the Grenadines, Surinam).

e. Southern Cone Common Market (Argentina, Brazil, Paraguay, Uruguay).

f. Economic and Monetary Community of Central African States (Cameroon, Central African Republic, Chad, Congo, Equatorial Guinea, Gabon).

g. Common Market for Eastern and Southern Africa (Angola, Burundi, Comoros, Democratic Republic of Congo, Egypt, Eritrea, Ethiopia, Kenya, Madagascar, Malawi, Mauritius, Namibia, Rwanda, Seychelles, Sudan, Swaziland, Uganda, Zambia, Zimbabwe). Before 2000, data unavailable for Namibia and Swaziland.

h. Economic Community of Central African States (Angola, Burundi, Cameroon, Central African Republic, Chad, Congo, Democratic Republic of Congo, Equatorial Guinea, Gabon, Rwanda, São Tomé and Principe).

i. Economic Community of Western African States (Benin, Burkina Faso, Cape Verde, Côte d'Ivoire, The Gambia, Ghana, Guinea, Guinea-Bissau, Liberia, Mali, Niger, Nigeria, Senegal, Sierra Leone, Togo).

j. Southern Africa Development Community (Angola, Botswana, Lesotho, Malawi, Mauritius, Mozambique, Namibia, South Africa, Swaziland, Tanzania, Zambia, Zimbabwe). Before 2000, data unavailable for Botswana, Lesotho, and Swaziland.

k. West African Economic and Monetary Union (Benin, Burkina Faso, Côte d'Ivoire, Guinea-Bissau, Mali, Niger, Senegal, Togo).

l. Association of Southeast Asian Nations/ASEAN Free Trade Area (Brunei Darussalam, Cambodia, Indonesia, Laos, Malaysia, Myanmar, Philippines, Singapore, Thailand, Vietnam).

m. Gulf Cooperation Council (Bahrain, Kuwait, Oman, Qatar, Saudi Arabia, United Arab Emirates).

n. South Asian Association for Regional Cooperation (Bangladesh, Bhutan, India, Maldives, Nepal, Pakistan, Sri Lanka).

o. Year of foundation.

painstaking investments in institution building. European countries have labored for more than half a century to build a wider web of political and diplomatic agreements designed to foster cooperation on monetary and financial matters. If European experience is any guide, then it may take years for East Asia to develop comparable arrangements and institutions. But another lesson from Europe is that the only way of reaching the destination is by starting down the path.

Second, building a cohesive regional grouping that entails the delicate project of exchange rate stabilization requires political will. For East Asian countries to create a regional monetary arrangement that even vaguely resembles the EMS, much less EMU, leadership will be required. China and Japan, as the two big countries in the region, are natural candidates to assume this role. But here long-standing rivalries complicate the prospects. So too does the fact that China is likely to grow considerably larger, and thus to exercise greater power in the region and globally, in the not-too-distant future. Be this as it may, if differences in their strategies and outlooks can be overcome, China and Japan together could provide formidable momentum to the process of monetary integration.[16]

East Asian Trade at the Crossroads

East Asia's strategy of export-led growth has resulted in the rapid expansion of its share of world trade. As shown in table 4-2, the region's share of global exports rose from 14 percent in 1980 to 19 percent in 1990 and 24 percent in 2003. Its share of global imports also rose from 14 percent in 1980 to 21 percent in 2003. Recent figures show, in contrast, that this increase has slowed since 2000. Thus East Asia's share of total world exports peaked at 24 percent in 2000 and then fell to 23 percent in 2001; it did not fully recover until 2003.[17]

A notable exception here is China. Whereas China's shares of total world exports and imports were far below those of Japan in 1980 (1 percent each for China versus 7 percent each for Japan), they have been rising rapidly, to the point where they have now reached levels comparable to Japan's.[18] The rapid growth of China's trade is all the more remarkable for the fact that the country's share of global GDP as of 2003 (at 3.9 percent) was still far less than that of Japan (at 11.8 percent).

East Asia's intraregional trade has also been rising. Overall, the percentage of intraregional exports in total exports in East Asia rose from 30 percent in 1980 to 42 percent in 2000 and 46 percent in 2003.[19] The key point in this context is that this rise is, again, almost entirely due to trade with China. China's share of South Korea's total trade, for example, rose from near zero in 1980 to 15 percent in 2003. By 2003, China had become the single largest

16. Sakakibara (2003) and Murase (2004) argue that the role of China and Japan in East Asia could be analogous to that of France and Germany in Europe. Similarly, the Kobe Research Project report submitted to the fourth gathering of the finance ministers of the Asia-Europe Meeting (ASEM Finance Ministers' Meeting) held in Copenhagen in July 2002 states that "It is essential for the Japan-China cooperation, as a core in East Asia, to lead the process of economic and financial integration, as the France-German alliance played a central role in the integration and cooperation process in Europe" (2002, p.16).

17. The East Asian share of global GDP shows the same pattern.

18. In 2003, China's share of total imports (5.3 per cent) finally surpassed that of Japan (4.9 percent).

19. The corresponding percentage of intraregional imports in total imports rose from 30.9 percent in 1980 to 48.1 percent in 2000 and 49.2 percent in 2003. ASEAN/Others already had relatively high intraregional shares in exports and imports in 1980, at 33.2 percent and 45.5 percent, respectively, but these shares rose further, to 53.3 percent and 60.9 percent, by 2003. Among the East Asian economies, Japan had the lowest share of intraregional trade, accounting for 39.2 percent of its combined imports and exports in 2003.

export market for South Korea, surpassing the United States. In the case of Japan, the United States remained about twice as important quantitatively as China as a destination for exports. But China was and continues to gain rapidly as a destination for Japanese exports. The same is true for many other East Asian countries.

Two potential explanations suggest themselves for why bilateral trade among other East Asian country pairs has tended to lag. First, exchange rate volatility has risen since the crisis of 1997–98. Before the crisis, most Asian countries maintained de facto dollar pegs, which worked to stabilize exchange rates within the region. With the adoption of more flexible exchange rates following the crisis, intraregional volatility has risen significantly. Econometric studies do not all agree, but the most recent studies tend to find a negative impact of such volatility on trade.[20]

Second, China, Japan, and South Korea have lagged in negotiating FTAs with their East Asian neighbors. Through the end of the 1990s, East Asia displayed a preference for open regionalism and multilateralism, as reflected in the objectives of Asia Pacific Economic Cooperation, or APEC, which encompassed members on the other side of the Pacific. This began to change only when the United States displayed a preference for regionalism and formed the North American Free Trade Area and when Europe cemented its single market with the introduction of the euro. East Asian countries have become increasingly proactive in negotiating bilateral and regional trade arrangements, although the effects may still be too recent to register clearly in the data.[21]

Table 4-3 summarizes existing FTAs along with others still at the negotiation and proposal stages. AFTA now includes the whole of Southeast Asia. In November 2001, China and the ASEAN countries agreed to form a free trade area within ten years, allowing for some preferential treatment for less developed ASEAN countries. Japan has concluded an FTA with Singapore and is negotiating a similar agreement with Korea and several individual ASEAN states. However, the prospect of a regionwide East Asian FTA covering all 13 ASEAN+3 countries remains remote mainly because China and Japan are continuing to pursue the bilateral route.

20. Clark (1975) and Hooper and Kohlagen (1978) argue that as exchange uncertainty rises, risk-adjusted profits fall and hence trade volume is lowered. Based on the argument of irreversible investment that is required to increase trade, Krugman (1989) also shows that exchange rate uncertainty gives rise to trade inertia. For recent surveys of this issue, see McKenzie (1999) and Clark and others (2004).

21. As shown in the empirical analysis that follows. Until the late 1990s, East Asian economies were involved with merely partial or loosely institutionalized groupings such as AFTA (ASEAN Free Trade Area) and APEC (Asia Pacific Economic Cooperation). In particular, the major three East Asian countries remained within the multilateral trade arrangements under GATT and the WTO.

Table 4-2. *East Asia's Global Trade Share, 1980–2003*[a]

Percent

Country or region	Exports						Imports						GDP					
	1980	*1990*	*2000*	*2001*	*2002*	*2003*	*1980*	*1990*	*2000*	*2001*	*2002*	*2003*	*1980*	*1990*	*2000*	*2001*	*2002*	*2003*
East Asia	13.8	19.1	24.0	22.7	23.5	23.8	14.0	17.3	20.4	20.0	20.3	20.5	13.9	18.7	22.6	20.9	19.5	19.7
Japan	7.1	8.5	7.5	6.6	6.5	6.3	7.4	6.7	5.8	5.5	5.1	4.9	9.6	14.0	15.4	13.3	12.2	11.8
Korea	1.0	2.0	2.7	2.4	2.5	2.6	1.1	2.1	2.4	2.2	2.3	2.3	0.6	1.2	1.5	1.5	1.1	1.7
ASEAN and others[b]	4.7	6.7	9.9	9.4	9.4	9.1	4.5	7.0	8.8	8.5	8.5	8.0	1.9	1.9	2.3	2.3	2.3	2.3
China	1.0	1.9	3.9	4.3	5.1	5.8	1.0	1.5	3.4	3.8	4.4	5.3	1.8	1.6	3.4	3.8	3.9	3.9
United States	12.5	11.6	12.1	11.9	10.8	9.6	13.4	14.7	18.8	18.5	18.1	16.7	24.9	26.4	31.2	31.9	32.0	30.0
European Union	42.5	44.8	37.8	39.7	40.3	41.4	45.7	44.4	37.2	37.9	38.0	39.2	25.5	25.4	19.2	19.6	20.5	22.5
Others	31.2	24.5	26.1	25.7	25.4	25.2	26.9	23.6	23.6	23.6	23.6	23.6	35.7	29.5	27.0	27.5	28.0	27.8

Source: United Nations, *Comtrade*, various years; International Monetary Fund, *Direction of Trade Statistics*, various years.

a. World totals add to 100 percent.

b. "ASEAN and others" includes ASEAN member countries such as Cambodia, Indonesia, Malaysia, Myanmar, Philippines, Singapore, Thailand, and Vietnam, and other NIEs, including Hong Kong, Macau, and Mongolia.

Table 4-3. *Major Free Trade Agreements for East Asian Countries, 1992–Present*

Agreement	*Status*	*Year initiated*
Bilateral FTAs		
Singapore-Japan	Effective	2002
China-Macao SAR	Effective	2003
China-Hong Kong SAR	Effective	2003
Japan-Philippines	Framework agreement signed	2004
Singapore-Korea	Effective	2004
Korea-Japan	Under negotiation	1998
Korea-Thailand	Joint study	2001
Japan-Thailand	Under negotiation	2002
Japan-Malaysia	Under negotiation	2002
Japan-Indonesia	Under negotiation	
"Plurilateral" FTAs		
AFTA[a]	Implemented	1992
ASEAN-China[b]	Framework agreement signed	2002
China-Japan-Korea	Joint study	2001
ASEAN-Korea	Under negotiation	2004
ASEAN-Japan CEP[c]	Signed	2002
ASEAN+3[d]	No formal discussion	

Sources: Lee and Shin (2004); authors' compilations.

a. AFTA is the ASEAN Free Trade Area.

b. ASEAN is the Association of Southeast Asian Nations.

c. CEP stands for Closer Economic Partnership

d. ASEAN+3 consists of ASEAN + China, Japan, and South Korea.

Will the East Asian countries ultimately form a unified free trade bloc? Outward orientation is an intrinsic component of the economic policy strategy of many East Asian countries, which bodes well for such an outcome. At the same time the region is highly diverse; countries range from the very large (China) to the very small (Brunei), from the very open (Singapore) to the relatively closed (Myanmar), and from the highly advanced (Japan) to the still predominantly agricultural (Laos). This diversity is impressive even by the standards of Europe, which is hardly a homogeneous continent. The very different circumstances of different East Asian countries are an obstacle that will have to be overcome if the region is to succeed in forging an integrated economic zone.

Deep integration will also require solving the exchange rate problem. If anything, this task has been rendered more complex by China's decision, in July 2005, to move to a regime of greater flexibility against the dollar. Exports to the

United States are important for East Asia, creating the dilemma of whether to stabilize vis-à-vis the dollar or vis-à-vis one or more regional currencies. However, East Asia's trade with the United States has tended to decline gradually as a share of the total. Assuming that this trend continues and the share of intraregional trade continues to grow, this dilemma may find a logical resolution.

Quantitative Analysis

Preceding sections highlighted two explanations for the stagnation of intraregional trade in East Asia: slow progress in concluding regional FTAs and rising intraregional exchange rate volatility. In this section we put these explanations to the test. We estimate the effect of regional FTAs on trade and ask whether exchange rate volatility has tended to neutralize their positive effects.

As noted above, the early empirical literature was generally unable to document a strong link between exchange rate volatility and the volume of trade. For example, studies in the mid-1980s by Padma Gotur and by Martin J. Bailey, George S. Tavlas, and Michael Ulan found that increased uncertainty about the exchange rate has no statistically significant impact on the volume of trade.[22] But more recent studies have turned up more evidence of a negative correlation.[23] In an influential study, Andrew Rose focuses on the extreme case where there is no uncertainty about the exchange rate: in other words, where a group of countries adopts a common currency.[24] His conclusion that membership in a currency union more than triples bilateral trade among member countries has attracted considerable attention. Those skeptical of Rose's conclusion question why the effect on trade is so large only at the extreme of zero volatility.[25] However, subsequent studies continue to show that the impact of a currency union on the volume of trade is significant and large, if not as large as in the original study. And Michael Klein and Jay Shambaugh, adopting a similar methodology, show that even fixed exchange rate regimes, despite not

22. Gotur (1985); Bailey, Tavlas, and Ulan (1986).

23. Bini-Smaghi (1991), Feenstra and Kendall (1991), Chowdhury (1993), Arize, Osang, and Slottie (2000), and Clark and others (2004) all found evidence of a negative relationship.

24. See Rose (2000).

25. In particular, his findings are based on cross-section data in which the share of countries in a currency union is about 1 percent. The countries in question tend to be relatively small, and many of them continue to trade heavily with their former colonial master (making it hard to determine whether the currency union effect is really a colonial legacy effect). Even if Rose's estimates are taken at face value, it is not clear how long it will take for a country joining a currency union to triple its trade with other member countries.

being a commitment as strong as that of a currency union, generate a large and significant effect on bilateral trade between the base country and other countries that peg to it.[26]

Here we revisit the relationship between exchange rate volatility and trade. In contrast to previous studies, we focus on the question of whether exchange rate volatility neutralizes the expected positive impact of FTAs on trade.

Our data cover 186 countries and the period 1973 to 1999.[27] The original data set has a measure for FTAs but covers only 11 agreements. We add data on 19 multilateral FTAs and 49 bilateral FTAs using information provided by the World Trade Organization (WTO). We also add a measure of exchange rate volatility by calculating the standard deviation of the monthly bilateral exchange rate for each year for each pair of countries.

We estimate a conventional gravity model of trade.[28] The dependent variable is the log volume of bilateral trade. In addition to the standard gravity variables, we include a dummy variable for participation in FTAs, an exchange rate volatility measure (calculated as described in the immediately preceding paragraph), and their interaction. We estimate this equation assuming, alternatively, random effects and country fixed effects. We also include a vector of year dummies.

Columns (1) and (2) of table 4-4 report results for the full sample. Column (1) shows the random effects estimates, while column (2) presents those estimated on the basis of fixed effects.

The gravity model fits the data well.[29] Of particular interest, the FTA coefficient is significantly greater than zero. The point estimate in column (1) suggests that joining an FTA increases trade between the partner countries by 43 percent.[30] Exchange rate volatility reduces trade: a one standard deviation rise in volatility reduces trade by 4 percent.[31]

26. Klein and Shambaugh (2004). Lee and Shin (2004) similarly find that both currency union and fixed exchange rate regimes boost trade, although the former has a larger effect than the latter.

27. The years before 1973 are not considered because most countries maintained fixed exchange rates, providing little variation in the key explanatory variable. Most of the variables are drawn from Rose (2004).

28. As in Glick and Rose (2002).

29. As predicted by the model, the log of GDP in pair, common land border dummy, common language dummy, current–colony colonizer dummy, and ex-colony colonizer dummy all have a positive and statistically significant relationship with the volume of trade between the two countries, while bilateral distance and log of area in pair have a significantly negatively relationship.

30. The increase in trade is estimated by applying the exponential function to the estimated coefficient of FTA: that is $e^{.348} = 1.426$.

31. This amounts to 8.7 per cent of the positive impact of FTAs on trade. In other words, by simply reducing exchange rate volatility by one standard deviation, a pair of countries can achieve 8.7 percent of the size of trade increases that are achieved by joining the same FTA.

Table 4-4. *Effects of Exchange Volatility on Trade Flows*[a]

	Full sample		*Europe*		*Asia*	
Variable	*Random effects (1)*	*Fixed effects (2)*	*Random effects (3)*	*Fixed effects (4)*	*Random effects (5)*	*Fixed effects (6)*
Log of distance	−1.255** (0.027)	—	−1.410** (0.093)	—	0.251 (0.308)	—
Log of GDP in pair	0.990** (0.011)	0.377** (0.031)	0.711** (0.032)	−0.202 (0.139)	1.746** (0.087)	0.788 (0.503)
Log of per capita GDP in pair	−0.167** (0.013)	0.058* (0.013)	−0.237** (0.037)	0.367** (0.144)	−1.480** (0.122)	−0.969 (0.505)
Log of area in pair	−0.158** (0.009)	—	0.218** (0.030)	—	−0.962** (0.074)	—
Common language	0.442** (0.055)	—	1.182** (0.271)	—	−0.208 (0.438)	—
Common land border	0.782** (0.140)	—	0.094 (0.195)	—	0.090 (0.501)	—
Ex-common colonizer	0.059 (0.070)	—	1.004** (0.318)	—	0.880 (0.516)	—
Ex-colony-colonizer	2.245** (0.181)	—	1.081** (0.382)	—	3.710** (1.258)	—
Current colony	−0.036 (0.201)	−0.040 (0.200)	—	—	—	—
Currency union	0.380** (0.092)	0.331** (0.100)	−0.147 (0.206)	−0.118 (0.194)	—	—
FTA	0.348** (0.034)	0.247** (0.035)	0.329** (0.026)	0.200** (0.026)	−0.706** (0.224)	−0.464* (0.233)
Volatility	−0.312** (0.034)	−0.301** (0.034)	−0.679** (0.094)	−0.689** (0.089)	−0.563 (0.428)	−0.104 (0.378)
FTA*volatility	0.111 (0.208)	−0.029 (0.208)	−0.610** (0.175)	−0.370* (0.166)	2.653 (1.387)	1.392 (1.265)
No. of observations	155,451	155,451	6,322	6,322	1,422	1,422
R-squared	0.591	0.507	0.802	0.106	0.576	0.031

Source: Authors' calculations.

a. The dependent variable is the log of real bilateral trade. In columns (1) and (2), panel data estimation techniques are applied to all annual observations over the period from 1974 to 1999. Columns (3) and (4) are based on a sample that includes only European countries. Columns (5) and (6) are based on a sample that includes only East Asian countries. Intercept and year dummy variables are included (not reported). Robust standard errors are reported in parentheses.

** Estimated coefficients are statistically significant at the 1 percent level.

* Estimated coefficients are statistically significant at the 5 percent level.

But while exchange rate volatility reduces trade directly, it does not seem to have any further indirect effect by mitigating the positive impact of FTAs. That is, the coefficient on the interaction term is not significantly different from zero.

The random effects estimates in column (2) remove any unobserved time-invariant country-pair specific factors, by construction.[32] Not unexpectedly, the coefficient indicating participation in an FTA is now smaller than before: the new point estimate now suggests that membership increases bilateral trade by 28 percent. The coefficient on exchange rate volatility is similar to before; again it implies that a one standard deviation increase in exchange rate volatility reduces trade by 4 percent. And, once more, the estimated coefficient of the interaction term between FTAs and exchange rate volatility is not statistically significant. An interpretation of these results is that while reducing exchange rate volatility is beneficial for trade integration, the motivation for pursuing exchange rate stability will be no stronger among FTA members, since the positive impact of FTAs on trade is independent of exchange rate volatility.

This last result is surprising insofar as the desire to promote intraregional trade is cited as part of the motivation for Europe's history of exchange rate stabilization agreements. Columns (3) and (4) therefore estimate the same equations for a subsample of European countries. The estimated coefficient on exchange rate volatility is twice as large as in columns (1) and (2) in absolute value terms and highly significant. More importantly, the interaction between FTAs and exchange rate volatility is now negative, large in absolute value, and statistically significant. Here a one standard deviation increase in exchange rate volatility reduces the impact of an FTA by half, from 103 to 49 percent (based on random effects estimation, or by an even larger ratio, from 59 to 17 percent, based on the fixed effects estimates).

Columns (5) and (6) report the same results for the sample of East Asian countries. Here the gravity equation fits the data less well. The coefficient of the log of distance is positive, not negative as expected, although it is not significantly different from zero. This reflects the fact that ASEAN members trade more with more distant East Asian countries, such as Japan and South Korea, than among themselves, as noted. (This may in turn reflect the operation of the supply chains and vertical intra-industry trade, as opposed to more traditional trade linkages, as emphasized in chapter 2 in this volume.) The FTA coefficient also has a counterintuitive (negative) sign that is statistically significant in both columns (5) and (6).[33] This is the AFTA effect, reflecting the fact that trade

32. The drawback of this procedure is that it is not possible to estimate the coefficients of other time-invariant control variables.

33. The results are somewhat different when, instead of stratifying the sample, an interaction term is used to identify the effect of the Asian FTA. The interaction term is positive and significant for the fixed

among ASEAN members was small relative to their trade with China, Japan, and South Korea. But most importantly, the interaction of exchange rate volatility with the FTA variable is not significant. This is consistent with the findings above for the full sample of countries. Again, there is no evidence for Asia that exchange rate volatility diminishes the benefits of moving to an FTA. Establishing a pan-Asian free trade area may create additional momentum for monetary integration, but only indirectly—if, for example, it encourages political solidarity among the participants, allowing the institutional obstacles to power sharing to be overcome—and not because currency stability is essential in order to reap the benefits of regional trade integration.

There are a number of reasons for interpreting these findings cautiously. For one thing, the effects of Asian FTAs are not particularly well estimated. That these effects disappear when the country sample is limited to Asia suggests that it is problematic to attempt to distinguish the effects of trade liberalization initiatives from the overwhelming growth of China's exports to and imports from its Asian neighbors. To put it another way, the full sample coefficients may be picking up market forces stimulating the growth of vertical intra-industry trade in the region—that is, the breakneck speed of China's export growth—rather than the effects of trade policy per se. For this reason, we prefer the full-sample estimates in columns (1) and (2), where the China effect is less dominant, to the results for the Asian subsample in columns (5) and (6).[34]

Conclusion

Regionalism in East Asia is taking two forms: free trade agreements and cooperation in monetary and financial affairs. The question, addressed in this chapter, is how the two processes fit together.

---

effect estimation, indicating that AFTA is creating trade as much as or more than other FTAs. Our results thus imply that AFTA is not creating trade only when compared to the trade among nonmembers in the same region.

34. Other reasons why the differential effects of Asian FTAs may not yet be visible include AFTA's exemptions for sensitive sectors and low-income countries. Implementation may be too recent to yet have a first order impact. (AFTA has been in effect among the five founding members of the Association of Southeast Asian Nations only since January 2002.) We would conjecture that with more time for regional liberalization to exert its effects, and once the three major countries in the region, China, Japan, and South Korea, begin to actively encourage the formation of regional FTAs, these anomalies may diminish and the contribution of exchange rate stability to trade integration may emerge. But this is a conjecture for the future. The key result for present purposes—namely the absence of a negative impact of exchange rate volatility on the effects of an Asian FTA—is robust.

Europe pursued trade integration first because, at the time, the Bretton Woods system provided the requisite level of exchange rate stability. But when Bretton Woods unraveled, the need arose for a regional initiative to buttress exchange rate stability, to which France and Germany responded with progressively deeper monetary cooperation. In North America, in contrast, trade integration has not created comparable momentum for regional exchange rate stabilization. The fact that the United States is an order of magnitude larger than both Canada and Mexico has made regional monetary negotiations problematic. The much larger U.S. economy is reluctant to share monetary control with its smaller neighbors, who in turn are reluctant to give over their monetary policy to the Federal Reserve Board. The North American situation is also different because of less political solidarity than in Europe and hence a more limited appetite for building transnational institutions.

Which example might East Asia follow? The growth in intraregional trade in East Asia is due primarily to the rise of bilateral trade between China and its neighbors. This suggests that China may eventually assume a position in East Asia not unlike that of the United States in the Western Hemisphere. This scenario does not bode well for monetary and financial cooperation, given the North American precedent. There is also less evidence than for Europe that exchange rate movements have a strong negative impact on the trade-creating effects of FTAs; in this respect as well, the Asian situation seems to resemble the North American case.

On the other hand, one can imagine that exchange rate fluctuations could grow more disruptive as the full effects of the AFTA, Asian bilaterals, and a prospective ASEAN+3 free trade area begin to be felt. One can also imagine an East Asia in which China and Japan are of roughly equal importance, at least for a period, and in which they provide the balance necessary for the negotiation of a durable monetary and financial arrangement. In this case they would play roles not unlike those historically assumed by France and Germany in Europe. This would require China and Japan to overcome their traditional historical enmity. However desirable, this would require a revolution in political thinking in both countries.

References

Arize, Augustine, Thomas Osang, and Daniel Slottje. 2000. "Exchange-Rate Volatility and Foreign Trade: Evidence from Thirteen LDCs." *Journal of Business and Economic Statistics* 18: 10–17.

Bailey, Martin J., George S. Tavlas, and Michael Ulan. 1986. "Exchange Rate Variability and Trade Performance: Evidence for the Big Seven Industrial Countries." *Weltwirtschaftliches Archiv* 122: 466–77.

Bini-Smaghi, Lorenzo. 1991. "Exchange Rate Variability and Trade: Why Is It So Difficult to Find Any Empirical Relationship?" *Applied Economics* 23: 927–35.

Chowdhury, Abdur. 1993. "Does Exchange Rate Volatility Depress Trade Flows? Evidence from Error-Correction Models." *Review of Economics and Statistics* 75: 700–06.

Clark, Peter B. 1975. "Uncertainty, Exchange Risk, and the Level of International Trade." *Western Economic Journal* 11: 302–13.

Clark, Peter B., Natalia Tamirisa, and Shang-Jin Wei, with Azim Sadikov and Li Zeng. 2004. "Exchange Rate Volatility and Trade Flows—Some New Evidence." International Monetary Fund (May).

Committee for the Study of Economic and Monetary Union. 1989. *Report on Economic and Monetary Union in the European Community (Delors Report)*. Office of Publications of the European Communities, Luxembourg.

Courchene, Thomas J., and Richard G. Harris. 2000. "North American Monetary Union: Analytical Principles and Operational Guidelines." Paper prepared for the conference on "Whether Canada and the U.S. Should Adopt a Common Currency." Western Washington University, Bellingham, Washington, April 30.

Eichengreen, Barry, and Alan M. Taylor. 2003. "The Monetary Consequences of a Free Trade Area of the Americas." Working Paper 9666. Cambridge, Mass.: National Bureau of Economic Research (May).

Feenstra, Robert C., and Jon D. Kendall. 1991. "Exchange Rate Volatility and International Prices." Working Paper 3644. Cambridge, Mass.: National Bureau of Economic Research (March).

George, Stephen. 1985. *Politics and Policy in the European Community*. Oxford, U.K.: Clarendon Press.

Glick, Reuven, and Andrew K. Rose. 2002. "Does a Currency Union Affect Trade? The Time-Series Evidence." *European Economic Review* 46: 1125–51.

Gotur, Padma. 1985. "Effects of Exchange Rate Volatility on Trade: Some Further Evidence." *IMF Staff Papers* 32: 475–512.

Grubel, Herbert G. 2000. "The Merit of a Canada–U.S. Monetary Union." *North American Journal of Economics and Finance* 11: 19–40.

Harrop, Jeffrey. 2000. *The Political Economy of Integration in the European Union*. Cheltenham, U.K.: Edward Elgar.

Hooper, Peter, and Steven W. Kohlagen. 1978. "The Effects of Exchange Rate Uncertainty on the Prices and Volume of International Trade." *Journal of International Economics*: 483–511.

Klein, Michael, and Jay Shambaugh. 2004. "Fixed Exchange Rates and Trade." Tufts University and Dartmouth College (August).

Kobe Research Project. 2002. *Report*. Institute for International Monetary Affairs, Tokyo (June) (www.mof.go.jp/jouhou/kokkin/tyousa/kobe_e.htm).

Krugman, Paul. 1989. *Exchange Rate Instability*. MIT Press.

Lee, Jong-Wha, and Kwanho Shin. 2004. "Exchange Rate Regimes and Economic Linkages." Korea University (September).

McKenzie, Michael D. 1999. "The Impact of Exchange Rate Volatility on International Trade Flows." *Journal of Economic Surveys* 13: 71–106.

Murase, Tetsuji. 2004. "The East Asian Monetary Zone and the Roles of Japan, China and Korea." Kyoto University.

Rose, Andrew K. 2000. "One Money, One Market: Estimating the Effect of Common Currencies on Trade." *Economic Policy* 30: 435–48.

———. 2004. "Do We Really Know That the WTO Increases Trade?" *American Economic Review* 94: 98–114.

Sakakibara, Eisuke. 2003. "Asian Cooperation and the End of Pax Americana." In *Financial Stability and Growth in Emerging Economies: The Role of the Financial Sector*, edited by Jan Joost Teunissen and Mark Teunissen, pp. 227–40. The Hague: Forum on Debt and Development.

Schweickert, Rainer. 2002. "The Making of European Monetary Union." In *Currency Union in East Asia*, edited by Choo Han Gwang and Yunjong Wang, pp. 39–80. Seoul: Korea Institute for International Economic Policy.

Shin, Kwanho, and Yunjong Wang. 2004. "Sequencing Monetary and Trade Integration." In *Exchange Rate Regimes in East Asia*, edited by Gordon de Brouwer and Masahiro Kawai, pp. 433–54. London: Routledge Curzon.

Volz, Ulrich. 2005. "Pegs, Baskets, and the Importance of Policy Credibility: Lessons of the 1992-93 ERM Crisis." Discussion Paper 323. Hamburg Institute of International Economics (June).

World Trade Organization (WTO). 2003. *World Trade Report 2003*. Geneva.

Wyplosz, Charles. 2001. "Regional Arrangements: Some Lessons from Postwar Europe." Paper prepared for conference on "The Role of Regional Financial Arrangements in Crisis Prevention and Management: The Experience of Europe, Asia, Africa, and Latin America." Forum on Debt and Development. Prague, June 21–22.

5 MASAHIRO KAWAI

Dollar, Yen, or Renminbi Bloc?

THE INTERNATIONAL MONETARY system in the post–World War II era underwent a dramatic transformation with the Nixon shock of August 1971, which suspended the convertibility of the U.S. dollar into gold. The preceding arrangement, called the Bretton Woods system or Bretton Woods-IMF regime, was based on fixed exchange rates against a dollar officially linked to gold. In the spring of 1973, the major industrialized countries adopted floating rates, allowing the value of their currencies to be determined in the market. Nonetheless, the U.S. dollar has remained the dominant international currency in the sense that many countries, including those in Asia, have continued to use the dollar as their nominal anchor and as the focal point for efforts at exchange rate stabilization. Although in the 1980s and 1990s the United States became the world's largest net foreign debtor as the result of a long string of current account deficits, the dollar's position as the dominant international currency was never seriously challenged.

In 1999 the international monetary system was again transformed, this time by the creation of a single European currency, the euro, by eleven Euro-

The author is grateful to Seok-Hyun Yoon for input and to Barry Eichengreen for constructive suggestions for improving the quality of this study. The findings, interpretations, and conclusions expressed are entirely those of the author and do not necessarily represent the view of the Asian Development Bank, its executive directors, or the countries they represent.

pean Union (EU) member countries.[1] The EU had completed its single market by 1993, constructing an integrated economic zone comparable to the U.S. economy in size. The majority of EU member states then adopted the euro, which began the process of transforming the world's international monetary system into a multi key-currency regime.

Meanwhile, other industrialized countries, such as Japan, the United Kingdom, Canada, and Australia, floated their currencies against the dollar and the euro. Some, like Canada, had already been floating for a considerable number of years. However, their currencies never acquired comparable international status.[2] The yen, in particular, has not functioned as a nominal anchor even in East Asia, despite nearly two decades of official efforts to promote its use.

The lack of regional integration in monetary affairs outside Europe creates an uneasy tension with the rapid integration of both product and financial markets. In East Asia, in particular, in recent years, there have been rapid advances in market-driven economic integration. China has recorded spectacular economic growth, raising the possibility that it may surpass Japan in economic size as early as 2015 (see figure 5-1). China is already the most important destination for the products of other East Asian economies and for foreign direct investment. The fast pace of Chinese growth understandably excites talk that the renminbi may ultimately emerge as yet another rival to the dollar in the international sphere, in East Asia in particular.

Motivated by these developments, this chapter poses three questions:

—Is there any evidence of a currency zone emerging in East Asia analogous to the integrated monetary area that has developed in Europe?

—If so, which regional currency will assume the dominant position: the Japanese yen, the Chinese renminbi, or a collection of currencies?

—And if Asian monetary integration is feasible, how might a future Asian monetary union come about?

The second section reviews the evolution of exchange rate arrangements in the principal East Asian economies. The third section then asks whether East Asia is an optimum currency area: that is, whether the economic preconditions are in place for the emergence of a single regional currency. The fourth section analyzes whether the renminbi might ultimately emerge as the dominant currency in the region. The fifth section discusses the challenges for monetary and

1. The number of member countries in the euro became twelve in 2001 with the participation of Greece, and thirteen in 2007 with the entry of Slovenia.

2. The U.K. pound sterling was once the dominant international currency but was eventually replaced by the U.S. dollar.

Figure 5-1. *GDP and per Capita GDP, the United States, the Core European Union, Japan, and China, 2000–50*

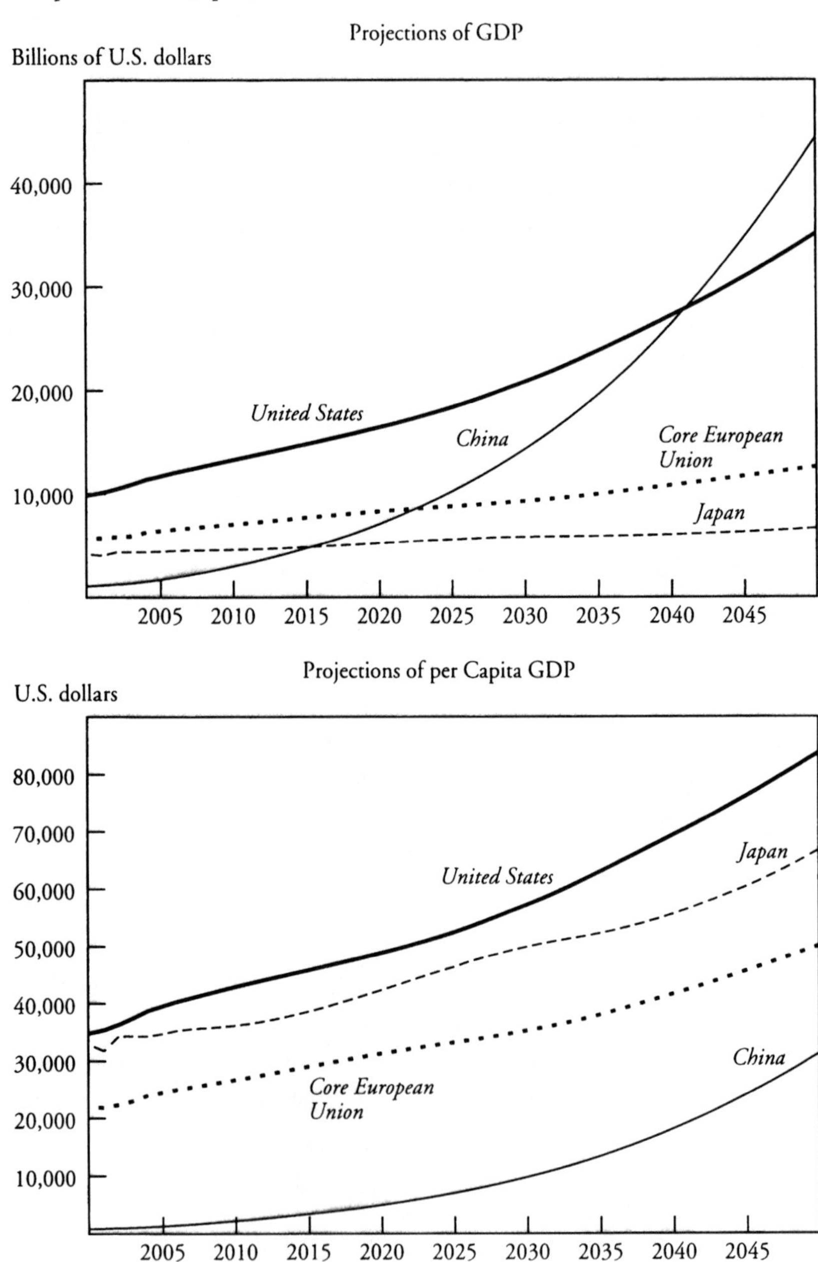

Source: Wilson and Purushothaman (2003).

exchange rate policy coordination and recommends policy steps to foster monetary integration. The sixth and final section concludes with some reflections on the broader policy implications.

Exchange Rate Arrangements in East Asia

Exchange rate arrangements in East Asia have evolved considerably since the crisis of 1997–98. This chapter focuses on the actual behavior of exchange rates, not so much on the officially declared regime. The literature on "fear of floating" argues that emerging markets that declare themselves as floating may continue to manage their exchange rates.[3] Thus in many countries observed exchange rate behavior may resemble a managed float or even a peg despite the fact that the declared regime is one of currency flexibility. Ronald McKinnon goes so far as to claim that fear of floating has caused the crisis-affected economies of East Asia to have all reverted to their pre-crisis dollar pegs.[4]

The discussion that follows examines the changing roles of the G-3 currencies—the U.S. dollar, the Japanese yen, and the euro (and its predecessor, the European Currency Unit, or ECU)—as anchors for exchange rate stabilization. I estimate regressions of daily movements in different East Asian exchange rates, expressed against the Swiss franc, on movements of the G-3 currencies.[5] The estimated coefficients can be interpreted as weights on the corresponding currencies in exchange rate policies, and the estimated standard error of regression can be interpreted as a measure of exchange rate volatility.

Regression Results

The basic results are summarized in table 5-1. For the pre-crisis period (January 1990 to June 1997) the estimated coefficients on the U.S. dollar are statistically significant and close to unity, the adjusted R^2 is close to 1, and the standard error of regression is small for all economies, but most especially for Hong Kong, South Korea, Indonesia, and Thailand.[6] These countries, clearly, were operating formal or informal dollar pegs. For other countries, the results are somewhat less decisive: the coefficient on the U.S. dollar and the adjusted

3. The seminal work on fear of floating is Calvo and Reinhart (2000).
4. See McKinnon (2005).
5. The methodology is that pioneered by Frankel and Wei (1993).
6. In Thailand, the speculative activity that had begun in 1996 and mounted in February and May 1997 clearly affected the currency movement before the outbreak of the baht crisis in July 1997.

Table 5-1. *Regression Results of Exchange Rate Movements for Emerging East Asian Economies: Pre-, Mid-, and Post-Crisis Periods*

Period (year/month)	*Constant*	*U.S. dollar*	*Yen*	*Euro*	*Adjusted* R^2	*Durbin-Watson*	*Standard error of the residual*	*N*
China (renminbi)								
1990/01–1991/06	0.000	1.023**	–0.036	0.011	0.7144	2.007	0.00517	390
1991/07–1992/12	0.000	1.045**	–0.040	–0.062*	0.8902	2.034	0.00319	394
1993/01–1994/06	0.001	0.967**	0.083	0.057	0.1157	2.007	0.01993	390
1994/07–1995/12	–0.000*	1.030**	–0.002	–0.030**	0.9829	2.082	0.00112	391
1996/01–1997/06	–0.000	1.019**	–0.010	–0.013	0.9337	2.833	0.00157	391
1997/07–1998/12	–0.000	0.996**	0.002	–0.003	0.9917	2.478	0.00060	393
1999/01–2000/06	0.000	1.004**	0.001	–0.015	0.9943	2.992	0.00052	391
2000/07–2001/12	–0.000	1.000**	–0.001	0.000	0.9999	1.988	0.00005	391
2002/01–2003/06	–0.000	1.010**	–0.002	–0.016	0.9870	2.921	0.00073	390
2003/07–2004/12	0.000	1.006**	–0.008	0.008	0.9756	2.841	0.00121	394
2005/01–2006/04	–0.000	0.963**	0.078**	0.000	0.9655	2.045	0.00114	343
South Korea (won)								
1990/01–1991/06	0.000	1.007**	–0.014	–0.018	0.9338	1.985	0.00214	390
1991/07–1992/12	0.000	1.029**	–0.015	–0.019	0.8102	2.003	0.00445	394
1993/01–1994/06	0.000	1.012**	–0.020*	0.002	0.9718	2.256	0.00121	390
1994/07–1995/12	–0.000	0.981**	0.080**	–0.041	0.9327	2.013	0.00221	391
1996/01–1997/06	0.000**	0.956**	0.065**	0.025	0.8584	1.804	0.00238	391
1997/07–1998/12	0.001	1.152**	0.044	0.092	0.0912	1.608	0.02430	393
1999/01–2000/06	–0.000	0.944**	0.065*	0.148	0.7472	1.692	0.00400	391
2000/07–2001/12	0.000	0.820**	0.304**	0.026	0.6639	2.527	0.00557	391
2002/01–2003/06	–0.000	0.760**	0.286**	–0.100	0.4867	2.549	0.00586	390
2003/07–2004/12	–0.000	0.806**	0.224**	0.060	0.7788	2.293	0.00397	394
2005/01–2006/04	–0.000	0.661**	0.267**	0.000	0.5815	2.316	0.00412	343

Cambodia (riel)								
1990/01–1991/06	0.004	0.517	–0.399	–0.151	–0.0028	2.011	0.04578	390
1991/07–1992/12	0.003	0.223	0.436	0.019	0.0055	2.042	0.04296	394
1993/01–1994/06	0.002	0.253	0.281	0.269	0.0090	2.023	0.03384	390
1994/07–1995/12	–0.001	0.881**	0.139	–0.292	0.0971	2.034	0.01922	391
1996/01–1997/06	0.000	0.954**	–0.152	–0.041	0.1120	2.088	0.01390	391
1997/07–1998/12	0.001	1.359**	0.145	–0.784**	0.1345	2.300	0.01935	393
1999/01–2000/06	–0.005	–3.145	–2.784	11.471	–0.0011	1.989	0.51854	391
2000/07–2001/12	–0.000	0.811**	0.020	0.314**	0.6028	2.574	0.00496	391
2002/01–2003/06	0.000	0.794**	0.024	0.013	0.7120	2.852	0.00325	390
2003/07–2004/12	0.000	0.773**	0.019	0.351**	0.6574	2.471	0.00467	394
2005/01–2006/04	0.000	0.860**	0.080	0.073	0.5267	2.271	0.00519	343
Hong Kong (dollar)								
1990/01–1991/06	–0.000	0.992**	–0.001	0.006	0.9973	1.570	0.00042	390
1991/07–1992/12	–0.000	0.997**	–0.010	0.009	0.9957	2.581	0.00059	394
1993/01–1994/06	–0.000	0.992**	0.001	0.009*	0.9974	2.178	0.00036	390
1994/07–1995/12	0.000	0.997**	0.000	0.003	0.9994	1.986	0.00021	391
1996/01–1997/06	0.000	0.998**	0.009**	–0.008	0.9977	2.588	0.00028	391
1997/07–1998/12	–0.000	1.001**	0.007*	0.001	0.9937	2.770	0.00053	393
1999/01–2000/06	0.000**	0.999**	0.001	0.003	0.9998	2.321	0.00011	391
2000/07–2001/12	0.000	0.999**	0.000	0.002	0.9999	2.159	0.00008	391
2002/01–2003/06	–0.000	1.000**	0.000	0.001	0.9996	2.248	0.00013	390
2003/07–2004/12	–0.000	0.982**	0.021**	0.001	0.9948	2.057	0.00055	394
2005/01–2006/04	–0.000	0.992**	0.028**	–0.054**	0.9899	2.835	0.00061	343

(continued)

Table 5-1. *Regression Results of Exchange Rate Movements for Emerging East Asian Economies: Pre-, Mid-, and Post-Crisis Periods (continued)*

Period (year/month)	*Constant*	*U.S. dollar*	*Yen*	*Euro*	*Adjusted* R^2	*Durbin-Watson*	*Standard error of the residual*	*N*
Indonesia (rupiah)								
1990/01–1991/06	0.000	0.956**	0.030	0.041	0.9098	2.073	0.00255	390
1991/07–1992/12	0.000**	1.002**	–0.005	–0.000	0.9901	2.290	0.00091	394
1993/01–1994/06	0.000*	0.997**	0.010	–0.007	0.9740	2.044	0.00116	390
1994/07–1995/12	0.000*	0.992**	–0.015	0.015	0.9709	1.998	0.00144	391
1996/01–1997/06	0.000*	1.010**	0.001	0.000	0.9370	2.164	0.00153	391
1997/07–1998/12	0.003	0.495	0.684*	–0.122	0.0144	1.960	0.05316	393
1999/01–2000/06	0.000	0.858**	0.258*	0.126	0.1810	1.794	0.01591	391
2000/07–2001/12	0.000	1.119**	0.022	0.198	0.2950	1.911	0.01261	391
2002/01–2003/06	–0.001	0.864**	0.091	0.002	0.4525	2.065	0.00630	390
2003/07–2004/12	0.000	0.817**	0.197**	0.039	0.6940	2.069	0.00488	394
2005/01–2006/04	–0.000	0.715**	0.144	0.154	0.3341	2.169	0.00685	343
Laos (kip)								
1990/01–1991/06	0.000	0.401**	0.132	0.059	0.0860	2.156	0.01328	390
1991/07–1992/12	0.000	0.217*	0.175	0.222**	0.1302	2.150	0.00982	394
1993/01–1994/06	0.000	0.427**	0.010	–0.017	0.1092	2.106	0.00837	390
1994/07–1995/12	0.001	0.786**	0.118	–0.165	0.1757	2.068	0.01313	391
1996/01–1997/06	–0.000	0.697**	–0.023	0.116	0.4025	2.101	0.00537	391
1997/07–1998/12	0.004*	0.779*	–0.223	–0.170	0.0125	2.154	0.03219	393
1999/01–2000/06	–0.005	–4.850	–4.077	15.924	–0.0003	1.989	0.72591	391
2000/07–2001/12	–0.000	0.775**	–0.009	0.063	0.4815	2.327	0.00569	391
2002/01–2003/06	0.000	0.794**	0.023	0.013	0.7716	2.852	0.00325	390
2003/07–2004/12	0.000	0.759**	0.012	0.332**	0.7016	2.582	0.00411	394
2005/01–2006/04	0.001	0.508**	0.015	–0.236	0.0314	2.013	0.01669	343

Malaysia (ringgit)								
1990/01–1991/06	0.000	0.908**	0.050**	0.067**	0.9524	2.518	0.00177	390
1991/07–1992/12	–0.000	0.889**	0.037	0.051**	0.9442	2.168	0.00205	394
1993/01–1994/06	0.000	0.896**	0.023	0.038	0.8284	1.501	0.00300	390
1994/07–1995/12	–0.000	0.865**	0.083**	0.017	0.9487	1.946	0.00175	391
1996/01–1997/06	–0.000	0.907**	0.044**	0.045	0.9222	1.959	0.00162	391
1997/07–1998/12	0.001	0.779**	0.364**	0.021	0.1693	1.878	0.01539	393
1999/01–2000/06	–0.000	1.004**	–0.003	0.011	0.9985	2.993	0.00027	391
2000/07–2001/12	–0.000	1.001**	–0.000	–0.001	0.9997	2.727	0.00012	391
2002/01–2003/06	–0.000	1.001**	–0.000	–0.004	0.9989	2.974	0.00021	390
2003/07–2004/12	0.000	1.002**	–0.003	–0.004	0.9986	2.992	0.00029	394
2005/01–2006/04	–0.000	0.972**	0.037	0.059	0.8479	3.043	0.00255	343
Philippines (peso)								
1990/01–1991/06	0.001	1.029**	0.038	0.006	0.6885	2.013	0.00576	390
1991/07–1992/12	–0.000	1.050**	–0.107	0.097	0.6705	1.994	0.00645	394
1993/01–1994/06	0.000	0.995**	–0.009	–0.067	0.6163	2.017	0.00537	390
1994/07–1995/12	–0.000	0.980**	0.060	–0.048	0.7797	2.222	0.00431	391
1996/01–1997/06	0.000	1.005**	–0.005	–0.004	0.9936	2.201	0.00047	391
1997/07–1998/12	0.001	0.879**	0.288**	–0.015	0.1889	1.717	0.01442	393
1999/01–2000/06	0.000	0.919**	0.085**	0.118	0.7429	1.957	0.00400	391
2000/07–2001/12	0.000	0.955**	0.026	0.035	0.3858	2.208	0.00876	391
2002/01–2003/06	0.000	0.867**	0.086*	0.088	0.6984	2.529	0.00383	390
2003/07–2004/12	0.000	0.923**	0.049	0.002	0.8594	2.621	0.00295	394
2005/01–2006/04	–0.000	0.865**	0.089*	–0.046	0.7937	2.264	0.00278	343

(continued)

Table 5-1. *Regression Results of Exchange Rate Movements for Emerging East Asian Economies: Pre-, Mid-, and Post-Crisis Periods (continued)*

Period (year/month)	*Constant*	*U.S. dollar*	*Yen*	*Euro*	*Adjusted* R^2	*Durbin-Watson*	*Standard error of the residual*	*N*
Singapore (dollar)								
1990/01–1991/06	–0.000	0.740**	0.084**	0.179**	0.8746	2.563	0.00274	390
1991/07–1992/12	–0.000	0.749**	0.126**	0.107**	0.9268	2.504	0.00221	394
1993/01–1994/06	–0.000	0.811**	0.080**	0.063*	0.887	2.475	0.00225	390
1994/07–1995/12	–0.000	0.787**	0.164**	–0.009	0.9177	2.263	0.00210	391
1996/01–1997/06	–0.000	0.790**	0.113**	0.104**	0.9285	2.229	0.00147	391
1997/07–1998/12	0.000	0.648**	0.353**	0.036	0.4293	2.200	0.00722	393
1999/01–2000/06	0.000	0.819**	0.124**	0.158*	0.8399	2.108	0.00280	391
2000/07–2001/12	0.000	0.777**	0.198**	0.048	0.8987	1.902	0.00229	391
2002/01–2003/06	–0.000	0.673**	0.299**	0.039	0.8683	2.316	0.00208	390
2003/07–2004/12	–0.000	0.640**	0.245**	0.189**	0.9175	2.298	0.00195	394
2005/01–2006/04	–0.000*	0.593**	0.308**	0.106	0.8666	2.197	0.00185	343
Taiwan (new Taiwan dollar)								
1990/01–1991/06	0.000	0.885**	–0.003	0.147	0.4516	2.869	0.00857	390
1991/07–1992/12	–0.000	0.986**	0.033	–0.066	0.6340	2.897	0.00681	394
1993/01–1994/06	0.000	0.988**	0.059	0.028	0.6662	2.877	0.00520	390
1994/07–1995/12	0.000	0.950**	0.065**	0.026	0.8957	2.020	0.00281	391
1996/01–1997/06	0.000	0.925**	0.018	0.041	0.9385	2.310	0.00143	391
1997/07–1998/12	0.000	0.877**	0.090**	0.051	0.6122	1.420	0.00495	393
1999/01–2000/06	–0.000	0.960**	–0.001	0.062	0.6971	2.769	0.00431	391
2000/07–2001/12	0.000*	0.982**	–0.015	0.063	0.8222	2.093	0.00323	391
2002/01–2003/06	0.000	0.898**	0.066**	–0.026	0.9195	1.896	0.00174	390
2003/07–2004/12	–0.000	0.902**	0.103**	0.023	0.8959	2.374	0.00254	394
2005/01–2006/04	–0.000	0.803**	0.152**	–0.012	0.7603	2.149	0.00298	343

Thailand (baht)								
1990/01–1991/06	0.000	0.955**	0.031*	0.034*	0.9545	2.073	0.00176	390
1991/07–1992/12	–0.000	0.960**	0.020	0.032**	0.9779	2.015	0.00134	394
1993/01–1994/06	–0.000	0.967**	0.012	0.015	0.9779	2.048	0.00105	390
1994/07–1995/12	0.000	0.875**	0.069**	0.052**	0.9883	2.399	0.00084	391
1996/01–1997/06	–0.000	0.832**	0.178**	0.137	0.4736	1.979	0.00618	391
1997/07–1998/12	0.001	0.608**	0.312**	0.100	0.1003	1.877	0.01722	393
1999/01–2000/06	0.000	0.824**	0.123**	0.166	0.5949	2.253	0.00532	391
2000/07–2001/12	0.000	0.823**	0.201**	0.058	0.7622	2.118	0.00400	391
2002/01–2003/06	–0.000	0.752**	0.207**	–0.014	0.6579	2.600	0.00392	390
2003/07–2004/12	–0.000	0.780**	0.219**	0.035	0.8978	2.116	0.00243	394
2005/01–2006/04	–0.000	0.691**	0.296**	0.112	0.7781	1.944	0.00280	343
Vietnam (dong)								
1990/01–1991/06	0.002*	0.528**	–0.072	–0.131	0.0530	2.226	0.01400	390
1991/07–1992/12	0.001	0.433**	0.121	–0.057	0.0613	2.101	0.01671	394
1993/01–1994/06	0.000	0.418**	–0.022	0.041	0.0907	2.026	0.00923	390
1994/07–1995/12	0.000	0.767**	0.039	–0.207**	0.4244	2.187	0.00649	391
1996/01–1997/06	–0.000	0.676**	–0.003	0.145	0.3902	2.287	0.00555	391
1997/07–1998/12	0.000	1.076**	0.081*	–0.387**	0.4563	2.598	0.00698	393
1999/01–2000/06	–0.000	0.913**	0.006	0.039	0.7773	2.903	0.00334	391
2000/07–2001/12	0.000	0.859**	–0.032	0.207**	0.7331	2.822	0.00366	391
2002/01–2003/06	0.000	0.799**	0.024	0.012	0.7272	2.856	0.00315	390
2003/07–2004/12	0.000	0.767**	0.055	0.263**	0.7884	2.733	0.00336	394
2005/01–2006/04	0.000	0.860**	0.030	0.187*	0.7929	2.907	0.00278	343

Note: Double asterisks (**) and a single asterisk (*) indicate that the estimated coefficients are statistically significant at the 1% and 5% levels, respectively.

R^2s are somewhat lower, while the standard error of the regression is higher. Overall, however, the results support the proposition that many emerging East Asian economies operated de jure or de facto dollar pegs before the crisis.

For some subperiods and in some countries, however, including South Korea, Singapore, Malaysia, and Thailand, the estimated coefficients of the Japanese yen are significant, although the point estimates rarely exceed 0.1. In this sense the yen played a rather limited role as part of a currency basket in the pre-crisis period. The euro (or more accurately, its predecessor, the ECU) also played a role in Singapore, Malaysia, and Thailand, according to these estimates.

For the crisis period (July 1997 to December 1998), the regressions for most East Asian economies show noticeable declines in U.S. dollar weights and adjusted R^2s. This decline is especially pronounced in Indonesia and Thailand, where the crisis had particularly disruptive effects on currency markets. (This is a reminder that it may be problematic to interpret patterns from this period as evidence of voluntary policy decisions. They may in fact be dominated by market pressures that the authorities had little ability to control, albeit more so for some countries than others; see discussion later in this chapter.) Although the point estimates for the dollar do not decline noticeably for South Korea, Malaysia, and the Philippines, the adjusted R^2 falls sharply, and the estimated standard error of the regression rises. According to these results, even countries not directly affected by the crisis like Singapore and Taiwan experienced declines in their U.S. dollar weights and adjusted R^2s. This is consistent with the qualitative evidence; in the case of Singapore, for example, the central rate was adjusted several times to weather the crisis. Nonetheless, these changes were not as pronounced as in the crisis-afflicted countries. In the extreme, management of the Hong Kong dollar and Chinese renminbi do not appear to have been noticeably affected by the turbulence in foreign exchange markets in this period.[7]

Along with these indications that the weight on the U.S. dollar declined in the crisis period, there is some evidence that weights on the yen rose, at least in Singapore, Indonesia, Malaysia, and Thailand. Only in South Korea and China are coefficients on the yen still statistically insignificant.[8] In contrast, it does not appear that the weights on the euro/ECU were noticeably affected by the crisis. This suggests that, all in all, the importance of the yen in the currency baskets of many countries rose during the crisis, while the importance of the euro/ECU did not.

7. Hong Kong was operating a rigid U.S. dollar-based currency board, while China refused to devalue against the dollar to avoid setting off another round of competitive devaluations in the region.

8. The same is true of Cambodia and Laos, but these are very special cases.

The results for the post-crisis period (January 1999 to April 2006) point to a growing diversity of exchange rate arrangements.[9] While a few countries returned to the pre-crisis pattern of a U.S. dollar–based exchange rate arrangement, others departed from it. Economies operating a stable dollar peg throughout the period, such as China and Hong Kong, continue to display dollar coefficients close to unity and adjusted R^2s close to one, while the estimated standard errors of the regression are even smaller than before. That Malaysia returned to a formal dollar peg arrangement in September 1998 is confirmed by the regression results. (China and Malaysia subsequently abandoned their pegs to the dollar in July 2005.)[10]

Indonesia is at the other extreme. Despite the fact that the coefficients on the U.S. dollar are close to unity in some post-crisis subsamples, the adjusted R^2 is lower and the standard error of the regression is higher than in the pre-crisis period. Evidently, the authorities have allowed the currency to fluctuate relatively widely against all potential anchor currencies, or at least they have been unable to prevent this despite frequent currency market interventions by Bank Indonesia to smooth the rupiah-dollar rate, in particular. Put another way, Indonesia has not been able to restore exchange rate stability despite interventions because of its difficult economic, social, and political problems.

Sandwiched between these two groups are countries that exhibit statistically significant U.S. dollar coefficients but point estimates that are smaller in size (the Philippines) or that are associated with lower adjusted R^2s (South Korea, Singapore, Thailand, and the Philippines). For these countries, the coefficient on the yen is on the order of 0.2 to 0.3 (except in the Philippines, where it takes on a lower value). Implied weights on the dollar tend to be noticeably lower than in the pre-crisis period. It is thus hard to argue that these countries have reverted to pre-crisis dollar-based exchange rate stabilization policies. But it is equally hard to argue that they have shifted to free floats. Their exchange rates are more flexible than in the pre-crisis period but more stable than those of the G-3 countries. South Korea and Thailand (and, to some extent, Taiwan) in particular appear to have shifted to de facto managed floating vis-à-vis a currency basket with relatively large weights on the dollar (on the order of 0.6 to 0.7) and smaller weights on the yen (on the order of 0.2 to 0.3). These countries' de facto baskets appear to be similar to that of Singapore, though the latter operates a managed float with a currency basket system based on a large number of currencies (while refusing to disclose the underlying weights).

9. See also Hernandez and Montiel (2003).

10. For more on this, see the discussion that follows and chapter 3 by Yu earlier in this volume.

Regime Changes in China and Malaysia

In July 2005, China revalued the renminbi by 2.1 percent against the dollar and moved from a de facto dollar peg to a managed float vis-à-vis an undisclosed basket of currencies. It was quickly followed by Malaysia, which adopted a similar exchange rate regime with a small initial revaluation. Hong Kong, in contrast, made no such move, instead sticking to its U.S. dollar-based currency board system. Even though China has shifted to a managed float with a maximum daily fluctuation of 0.3 percent vis-à-vis the U.S. dollar, actual daily movements have remained strictly limited, and the weight assigned to the dollar in the currency basket (not officially announced by the authorities) is apparently close to unity.[11]

In a context where there were fears of overheating, revaluation of the exchange rate was considered desirable because it would support the authorities' efforts to tighten the credit market conditions. The currency was considered undervalued because of the rapid pace of foreign exchange reserve accumulation, the growth of the trade surplus, and unsustainably rapid growth of the economy. Purchasing power parity (PPP) calculations adjusted for Balassa-Samuelson effects suggest that the renminbi is undervalued to a significant degree. The currency's deviation from the Balassa-Samuelson fitted curve in a figure with per capita income (valued at the PPP U.S. dollar) on the horizontal axis and the exchange rate deviation from PPP on the vertical axis, for a sample of some 150 countries, was on the order of 40 percent in 2004. The same conclusion follows from data on reserve accumulation. China's foreign exchange reserves rose from $30 billion in 1990 to $168 billion in 2000 and to $822 billion at the end of 2005 and are expected to surpass $1 trillion in 2006—at which point they will exceed those of Japan. This indicates that the renminbi would have been appreciating had the authorities not been intervening.[12]

But the July 21 revaluation against the dollar was small, and the renminbi's subsequent movements were limited. The Chinese authorities may believe that the economy is not ready to absorb large exchange rate fluctuations because of

11. The results of table 5-1 suggest that the U.S. dollar coefficient for the renminbi is somewhat lower than unity and the yen coefficient is positive for the period January 2005–April 2006. But if the July 21 observation is excluded, the estimated coefficients are 1.000 for the dollar and 0.003 (statistically insignficant) for the yen, thereby indicating that the renminbi basically follows a de facto U.S. dollar-stabilization system with a gradual trend appreciation. A number of authors have also estimated Frankel-Wei regressions on renminbi data for the post-July 21 period. Eichengreen (2006) does so on data through March 2006. He is unable to reject the null of a coefficient of unity of the dollar, the null of coefficients of zero on the other major currencies, and no trend in the implicit basket weights.

12. For a more extensive review of the evidence on renminbi undervaluation, see Frankel (2005).

the underdeveloped nature of its money markets and the consequent paucity of currency hedging instruments. In addition, because of tight capital and exchange controls, the authorities still enjoy some monetary autonomy without having to resort to greater exchange rate flexibility.

While there have been limited immediate effects of the exit of the renminbi and the Malaysian ringgit from their de facto U.S. dollar pegs, these events have important potential consequences. As China and Malaysia gravitate toward greater exchange rate flexibility, their central banks will be able to use monetary policy more easily for macroeconomic stabilization. (Malaysia began to move in this direction in early 2006.) These moves will make it easier for other East Asian economies to then similarly introduce greater exchange rate flexibility; thus further slowing the pace of reserve accumulation and precipitating the end of the so-called "revived Bretton Woods system."[13] Greater exchange rate flexibility could also contribute to the correction of global payments imbalances, assuming of course that the United States also takes appropriate policy measures. Finally, the shift to a basket-based managed float could facilitate the coordination of exchange rate policies in East Asia, encouraging still other countries to move to similar exchange rate arrangements, and thereby restoring the common exchange regime that was previously characteristic of the region.

Summary of Current Exchange Rate Arrangements

Table 5-2 summarizes exchange rate arrangements in East Asia as of mid-2006 based on the preceding analysis. Japan is the only country that operates an arrangement close to a pure float—although the Bank of Japan has intervened periodically in the foreign exchange market.[14]

At the other end of the spectrum, Hong Kong and Brunei have currency board systems by which they stabilize against the U.S. dollar and Singapore dollar, respectively. Other countries have intermediate arrangements ranging from managed floats with relatively extensive exchange rate flexibility (Indonesia, Laos, and Cambodia) to managed floats with relatively limited flexibility (Singapore, Thailand, the Philippines, Taiwan, South Korea, and Vietnam). Finally there are countries that appear to be in the process of navigating a transition to greater flexibility, although in practice it seems that they are still strongly wedded to their de facto dollar pegs (China and Malaysia). Singapore

13. Both the concept and the phrase originate with Dooley, Folkerts-Landau, and Garber (2005).

14. Between the beginning of 2003 and March 2004, the Bank of Japan intervened heavily in the currency market, accumulating $355 billion of foreign exchange reserves to prevent rapid appreciation of the yen. Since mid-March 2004, the Bank of Japan has not intervened in the market.

Table 5-2. *Exchange Rate Arrangements in East Asia, 2004–06*[a]

Exchange rate arrangement	*Countries/de jure arrangement*
Free float	Japan (independent float)
Intermediate arrangement	
Managed float with large rate flucuations	Cambodia (managed float)
	Indonesia (managed float)
	Laos (managed float)
Floating with limited rate fluctuations	Korea (independent float)
	Philippines (independent float)
	Singapore (managed float)
	Taiwan (managed float)
	Thailand (managed float)
	Vietnam (managed float)
	Malaysia (managed float)
Floating with very limited rate fluctuations (de facto peg to U.S. dollar)	China (conventional fixed peg)
Hard peg	Brunei (currency board peg to Singapore dollar)
	Hong Kong (currency board peg to U.S. dollar)

Source: Author's compilations.

a. This table summarizes de facto exchange rate arrangements in place by taking into account the arrangements reported by IMF, *Annual Reports on Exchange Arrangements and Exchange Restrictions, 2005.* Note that China and Malaysia moved from a fixed peg to a managed float midway through 2005. Malaysia then moved to a flexible rate in early 2006, which is where I group it here.

operates a formal currency basket arrangement, while Thailand, Korea, and, to some extent, Taiwan are shifting to de facto currency basket systems. No East Asian economy—apart from Hong Kong—is on a formal U.S. dollar peg. Thus while there is some evidence of continued dollar pegging, McKinnon's thesis of a revived dollar standard embracing the entire East Asian region is too strong.

That a number of countries have moved away from the so-called East Asian dollar standard is not surprising. Although some degree of exchange rate stability is desirable for emerging East Asia, there have been clear problems with using the U.S. dollar as the sole anchor currency. Currencies that were de facto tied to the dollar became overvalued on an effective basis from mid-1995 due to both higher domestic inflation than in the United States and the dollar's appreciation vis-à-vis the major industrialized currencies, particularly the yen and the deutsche mark. With the dollar's appreciation, emerging East Asia saw its price competitiveness deteriorate and economic activity begin to slow. These developments, and therefore the currency regime, were at least contributing factors to the Asian crisis.

In addition, with the volatility of the yen-dollar exchange rate (and, in the future, one presumes, the renminbi-dollar rate), the benefits of a dollar-based exchange rate regime will be more limited. Using the dollar as the sole anchor is problematic given that emerging East Asia has developed diverse economic relationships, through trade, foreign direct investment (FDI) flows, and other forms of capital flows, with the United States, Japan, and the European Union alike. For much of emerging East Asia, the United States is no longer the dominant economic partner. Rather, the relative importance of Japan and the European Union is as large and in some cases larger. These diverse economic linkages suggest that exchange rate management exclusively vis-à-vis the dollar is now less than ideal for ensuring stability.

A dollar-euro-yen basket would more effectively buffer emerging East Asia against yen-dollar and dollar-euro volatility. Weights in the basket need not be uniform across East Asian countries, at least initially. They could depend on the relative importance of the G-3 countries as trading partners and sources of FDI and on the attractiveness of holding the dollar, yen, and euro as international reserves.[15] How strictly countries peg to this basket should depend in each case on a country's conditions and preferences.

Eventually, the adoption of similar currency baskets by different East Asian countries and loose stabilization vis-à-vis that basket would enhance the stability of both effective and intraregional exchange rates. These benefits would be particularly large for members of the Association of Southeast Asian Nations, or ASEAN (Brunei, Cambodia, Indonesia, Laos, Malaysia, Myranmar, the Philippines, Singapore, Thailand, and Vietnam), who reduced their intraregional tariffs on manufacturing products to a maximum of 5 percent in early 2002, completing the initial phase of the ASEAN Free Trade Agreement. Preventing wide swings in exchange rates among ASEAN countries would help to further deepen their free trade area.[16] Initial steps in this direction would not require formal agreements on common baskets or frequent, concerted joint actions in foreign exchange markets. At the outset countries would only have to choose similar baskets.[17]

15. This last factor would depend in turn on expectations of the trend in the yen–dollar exchange rate, on the success of the euro, and on the internationalization of the yen.

16. As documented by Shin and Wang in chapter 4.

17. This proposal has some parallels with Gongpil Choi's scheme for an Asian Exchange Rate Mechanism, discussed in chapter 6 in this volume.

Is East Asia an Optimum Currency Area?

If price and wage flexibility is limited, then flexible exchange rates become important for adjustment. This is the insight of Milton Friedman's classic argument for floating exchange rates.[18] In contrast, Robert Mundell and Ronald McKinnon argued that fixed exchange rates can produce better outcomes even without price and wage flexibility.[19] Mechanisms supported by a common monetary policy can facilitate adjustment so long as the disturbances impinging on different countries are symmetric, while fiscal transfers and labor mobility can do the job for asymmetric shocks. The reduction in uncertainty delivered by exchange rate stability can be important for facilitating foreign trade, investment, and financial transactions. In this view, pegged rates are appropriate for a group of economies that are closely integrated with one another and subject to similar economic shocks. The resulting economic zone is commonly referred to as an optimum currency area (OCA).

Subsequent contributions to OCA theory have further elaborated the conditions under which a group of economies is better off adopting permanently fixed exchange rates vis-à-vis one another or issuing a common currency.[20] These include:

—Openness to other members of the area

—Product, factor, and financial market integration

—Symmetry of the shocks affecting area members

—Similarity of preferences over output-inflation trade-offs

—Willingness and ability to coordinate economic policies.

Similarly, the benefits of forming a currency area take the following forms:

—Avoidance of exchange rate volatility and misalignments and the associated reduction of uncertainty

—Improved cross-border price transparency, leading to more intense competition

—Deeper and better integrated financial markets

—Reduced need to hold national foreign exchange reserves.

On the cost side of the ledger is the loss of monetary autonomy: that is, the elimination of an independent monetary policy useful for responding to country-specific shocks.

18. In Friedman (1953).

19. In Mundell (1961) and McKinnon (1963).

20. See Kawai (1987) and Tavlas (1993). This section draws on Kawai and Motonishi (2005b).

With economic integration, the benefits of exchange rate stability will rise relative to the costs.[21] Shocks will become more symmetric.[22] There will be more scope for cross-border competition. This implies that once a group of economies has achieved a certain level of intragroup integration, they are better off fixing their exchange rates and even adopting a common currency.

Effects of Regional Integration

In East Asia, economic interdependence has deepened as a result of market-driven activities related to trade, investment, and finance. Thanks to the World Trade Organization (WTO), its predecessor the General Agreement on Tariffs and Trade (GATT), and Asia Pacific Economic Cooperation (APEC), cross-border transactions in goods, services, and FDI have expanded enormously. Cross-border portfolio investment and bank-intermediated flows have also grown. Given proximity that promotes natural linkages, the removal of regulatory barriers to cross-border transactions has progressively strengthened trade, investment, and financial integration among the East Asian economies.[23]

The international division of labor that has emerged as a result of these dynamics has promoted vertical intra-industry trade in capital goods, parts and components, intermediate goods, and semi-finished and finished products.[24] These trends accelerated in the wake of the Plaza Accord in 1985, when Japanese multinational firms, compelled by the sharp appreciation of the yen to relocate their production bases abroad, began building regional production networks centered on ASEAN. Not just multinational corporations from developed economies (Japan, the United States, and the members of the European Union) but also firms from East Asia's newly industrializing economies (that is, Hong Kong, Singapore, South Korea, and Taiwan) and from middle-income ASEAN countries like Malaysia and Thailand all provide FDI, thus working to weave a web of regional supply chains centered on China. Intraregional transactions now account for 55 percent of East Asia's trade. The intensity of regional trade as conventionally measured is comparable to, or even greater than, that in the European Union and North America. While the

21. As argued by Krugman and Obstfeld (2003), among others.

22. The most influential evidence in favor of this conclusion is Frankel and Rose (1998).

23. For more on East Asian economic interdependence, see Kawai (2005a, 2005b) and Kawai and Motonishi (2005a).

24. See also chapter 2 by Yoshitomi for discussion and documentation of these trends.

development of this regional production network has been premised on the existence of U.S. and European markets, its dependence on these outside markets will decline as demand for final products within the East Asian region continues to grow.

The growth of FDI inflows to emerging East Asia has been even more remarkable. The share of emerging East Asia in global FDI inflows rose from 8 percent in 1985 to 25 percent in the mid-1990s, before declining to 20 percent in 2004. China is the largest emerging market recipient of FDI inflows. The country has benefited enormously from participating in regional supply chains and from becoming the assembly platform for producers of consumer goods throughout the region, neither of which would have been possible without substantial amounts of inward FDI. More recently, substantial quantities of FDI have begun to flow to other relatively low-income Asian countries such as Vietnam. Still other less developed East Asian economies will presumably follow in their train.

Relative to trade and FDI, financial integration has been less dramatic, since several countries, most notably China, still maintain a range of financial restrictions and capital controls. But here too, phased liberalization is ongoing. Cross-border operations by developed country commercial banks and foreign portfolio investment by institutional investors have significantly strengthened linkages among regional financial markets. The WTO membership of the region's more advanced countries has compelled them to relax a range of financial services restrictions and to remove barriers to the entry of foreign banks. One result has been the increasingly tight co-movement of regional interest rates and stock prices. In a less positive way, the speed, scale, and extent of the contagion of the Asian financial crisis itself attested to the development of financial linkages in the region.

Another consequence of these linkages is heightened macroeconomic interdependence. GDP, personal consumption, and fixed investment have all become increasingly synchronized across countries. Table 5-3 shows correlation coefficients between the first principal components of each major East Asian economic variable and the corresponding country variables.[25] It is clear that the activity variables are highly correlated within major economies in East Asia, China being a notable exception.[26] Activity variables in East Asia are more closely correlated with those of Japan than with those of the United States,

25. The first principal component is essentially a linear combination of the different underlying time series for each country. The values shown in the table thus summarize co-movements of economic variables between East Asia as a group and the individual countries, including non-East Asian economies.

26. While this result is based on historical data, China is bound to have a strong intraregional correlation sooner or later as its economy advances in marketization and international integration.

Europe, Australia, and India. Surprisingly, U.S. real activity variables are not significantly correlated with East Asia's first principal component. On the other hand, inflation rates in East Asia are equally highly correlated with those of the United States, Europe, and Japan. In terms of real variables, then, emerging East Asia is more tightly linked with Japan than with the United States, whereas in terms of nominal variables the extent of emerging East Asian linkages with Japan and the United States is roughly equal.

Labor market integration is not so pronounced, notably in Northeast Asia. South Korea and Japan have maintained tight restrictions over immigration. However, labor mobility is surprisingly high in Southeast Asia, particularly among Malaysia, Singapore, and Thailand. In 1994 Junichi Goto and Koichi Hamada presented early evidence that labor mobility in Southeast Asia was already as high as that in Europe.[27] Barry Eichengreen and Tamim Bayoumi note that labor markets are more flexible in East Asia than Europe, as measured by both the cyclical variability of wages and flows in and out of employment.[28] If speed of adjustment to shocks is faster in East Asia, as would appear to be indicated by this evidence, then the cost of permanently fixing the exchange rate and forgoing monetary policy autonomy may be lower. Looking forward, efforts to craft bilateral free trade agreements in the region should further stimulate labor mobility, particularly between Southeast and Northeast Asia.

In sum, interdependence among East Asian economies has risen to a level almost comparable to that in Europe at the beginning of the 1990s when the European Union embarked on its transition to monetary union. A subgroup centering on Japan, Malaysia, Singapore, South Korea, Taiwan, and Thailand is coming increasingly close to satisfying the optimum currency area criteria. More broadly, the heightened interdependence of regional economies provides a further argument for stabilizing intraregional exchange rates. Given weak interdependence with U.S. business cycles, it may be argued that these East Asian economies should aim to stabilize intraregional exchange rates through policy coordination rather than by pegging to the dollar. The ultimate goal of this process, one imagines, might be the creation of an Asian common currency.[29]

Endogeneity of Optimum Currency Area Criteria

Skeptics of Asian exchange rate policy coordination might still argue that intraregional exchange rate stabilization is inadvisable because of the lack of

27. See Goto and Hamada (1994).
28. In Eichengreen and Bayoumi (1999).
29. Kuroda (2004) argues for the creation of a single Asian currency.

Table 5-3. *Correlation Coefficients between First Principal Component Scores for East Asia and Individual Country Data, 1980–2002*[a]

Countries and regions[b]	*GDP*	*Personal consumption*	*Gross fixed investment*	*Real share prices*	*Real effective exchange rate*	*GDP deflator*	*CPI*	*WPI*
United States	0.01	–0.32	–0.41	0.36	0.48	0.17	0.85	0.30
EU-15	0.01	–0.18	–0.14	0.33	–0.33	0.10	0.78	–0.01
Australia	–0.16	–0.15	–0.20	0.33	0.67	–0.02	0.31	0.00
New Zealand	0.27	–0.04	0.19	0.11	0.27	–0.07	0.40	0.22
India	0.09	0.01	–0.03	0.10	0.40	0.06	0.63	0.34
Japan	0.58	0.39	0.41	0.71	–0.26	0.15	0.90	0.46
Korea	0.71	0.78	0.67	0.86	0.70	0.27	0.89	0.48
China	0.07	–0.14	–0.26	. . .	0.43	–0.40	0.15	. . .
Taiwan	0.51	0.28	0.28	0.71	0.72	0.35	0.85	0.50
Hong Kong	0.74	0.63	0.58	. . .	0.48	–0.06	0.80	. . .
Singapore	0.77	0.76	0.59	. . .	0.77	0.08	0.87	0.45
Malaysia	0.90	0.87	0.95	. . .	0.81	0.40	0.79	0.68
Thailand	0.89	0.92	0.88	. . .	0.80	0.54	0.87	0.70
Philippines	0.33	0.31	0.55	0.91	0.81	–0.06	0.57	0.27
Indonesia	0.89	0.65	0.89	. . .	0.86	0.99	0.21	0.92

Source: Adapted from Kawai and Motonishi (2005a, table 5).

a. The figures are correlation coefficients between the first principal component scores for East Asia and the original, log first-differenced series of individual countries. Personal consumption and gross fixed investment are at constant prices. Share prices are similarly deflated by the GDP deflator.

b. In this analysis, East Asia includes China, Japan, and South Korea, as well as Hong Kong, Indonesia, Malaysia, the Philippines, Singapore, Taiwan, and Thailand.

labor market integration, economic and structural convergence, and fiscal policy coordination across countries. One objection to this view is that the optimum currency area criteria are endogenous. Once a group of countries permanently fixes its exchange rates, the degree of intra-area economic integration will rise, and shocks will become more symmetric. One need not worry too much, then, about the OCA criteria, since these will obtain endogenously. This view is based on the finding that when a country fixes its exchange rate against the currency of another, there tends to be a significant increase in trade and investment flows between the two, and greater trade and investment flows are associated empirically with stronger business cycle co-movements.

The endogeneity of OCA criteria implies that countries fixing their exchange rates or contemplating the formation of a common currency area do not have to achieve the requisite levels of openness, integration, and symmetry of shocks in advance. Only political commitment is required. If this exists and if as a result a group of countries succeeds in fixing its exchange rates or adopting a common currency, then the conditions needed for this to be a happy state of economic affairs will be created endogenously.

If this is correct, then the most important factor is the region's "political will" for closer exchange rate policy coordination. A combination of such a political will and the observation that the OCA conditions have been increasingly fulfilled in the region in a way comparable to the European Union (EU) does reinforce the case for intraregional exchange rate stabilization. While China is not yet part of this optimum currency area, it too is being increasingly integrated with other East Asian economies through trade and FDI. Hence it will be useful to establish a stable relationship between the Chinese renminbi and the ASEAN currencies.

There are two practical means of stabilizing exchange rates among East Asian currencies. One is for each country to peg its currency to a common key currency or a common basket. The other is by creating a multilateral system similar to the Snake and Exchange Rate Mechanism (ERM) in Europe. Given that economic, and particularly structural, convergence among East Asian countries is not yet tight and that political relationships are not sufficiently mature to support the creation and maintenance of a tightly coordinated multilateral arrangement, the second approach would be difficult. The first, by comparison, would appear to be more realistic.

The question is which currency or basket of currencies East Asian governments should select as their external anchor. Past practice has been to peg to the dollar as a way of indirectly stabilizing intraregional rates. But the drawbacks of this East Asian dollar standard were underscored by the Asian crisis, as noted above. For countries with strong economic ties to Japan, pegging to the dollar meant volatility against the yen.[30] Many East Asian economies exhibit low business cycle co-movements with the United States, something that appears to reflect deep structural factors that will be difficult to change. Pegging to the yen may be preferable for these countries insofar as cyclical co-movements with Japan are greater.

The problem is that Tokyo is not a world-class financial center. In the absence of sufficiently liquid markets, pegging to the yen or holding yen balances would not be an attractive option. Thus a reasonable compromise would be for the yen and the dollar to share the anchor currency role.

What Role for China in Regional Monetary Integration?

Extrapolating current trends suggests that China could surpass Japan in economic size as early as the mid-2010s and the United States by the mid-2040s.[31] This overtaking scenario might not come to pass for any number of reasons, including macroeconomic and financial turbulence, resource, energy, and environmental constraints, and political and social instability. But even taking such factors into account, there is still good reason to think that China's aggregate GDP will exceed those of Europe, Japan, and even the United States sometime in the twenty-first century, given its economic potential and the sheer size of its population.

These observations raise the question of whether the renminbi might eventually rival the dollar, the euro, and the yen as an international currency and whether it could serve as the anchor for an East Asian monetary arrangement. In fact, this is unlikely to be the case for the foreseeable future. In order for China's currency to be widely held and utilized in third countries, its economy must become fully open with respect to trade, investment, and finance. It was the openness and liquidity of U.S. financial markets, after all, that encouraged the architects of the Bretton Woods system to institutionalize the dollar's asymmetric role and that were responsible for the singular willingness of foreign investors to hold dollar-denominated assets. If the renminbi is to play a significant role as an international currency, China must similarly encourage global investors to freely hold and utilize it by liberalizing its capital account, removing its exchange controls, and building deeper and more

30. For evidence see Kwan (2001).
31. Wilson and Purushothaman (2003) flesh out this assumption.

liquid financial markets. Practically speaking, this is not going to happen anytime soon. A precondition for capital account convertibility is that the country must complete its transition to market economy status and establish a sound and resilient financial sector. China is still far from a free market economy, the problems in its banking system are extensive, and its capital markets are underdeveloped. At a minimum, completing this transition will require another ten to twenty years. After that it will take time for international investors to adapt themselves to the new situation and significantly reconfigure their portfolios.[32]

Moreover, while per capita incomes in China may rise substantially—to a fifth or even a third those of Japan, Europe, and the United States by 2050—the country will still face enormous challenges in reducing poverty, limiting income inequality, and completing a peaceful democratic transition. Until these tasks are completed and China's economic, social, and political transition is consolidated, it is hard to imagine that investors in global and regional markets will feel comfortable using the renminbi as extensively as the dollar, euro, and yen.

Finally, even if the renminbi does acquire international currency status, there is the question whether it will supplant the dollar's role in East Asia. The answer depends as much on economic developments in the United States as on events in China itself. Unless the U.S. economy experiences serious difficulties, causing the advantages of incumbency to be squandered, it will be hard for the renminbi to break the hold of the dollar. Incumbency is an advantage in reserve currency competition, and the dollar has been the incumbent currency.

None of this precludes the possibility that the renminbi may begin to function as an international currency for smaller countries closely linked to China such as Hong Kong, Laos, Mongolia, and Myanmar. Already there are signs of this beginning to happen.[33] But this is different from saying that it can serve as the anchor for a regional exchange rate system.

Steps toward Asian Monetary Integration

The upshot is that no single currency is an ideal anchor for East Asia as a whole. There is an argument, therefore, that emerging East Asia should seek currency

32. For more on this, see the discussion later in this chapter.

33. The renminbi is used and held in Hong Kong and Mongolia and the northern part of Laos and Myanmar, which are physically closest to China. Such tendencies will presumably spread as China continues to grow.

stability by adopting a currency basket composed of the yen, the dollar, and the euro—but excluding the renminbi for the time being because of its lack of convertibility. Japan for its part might maintain its current floating system and allow the yen to act as one of the G-3 anchor currencies.

If emerging East Asian economies stabilize their currencies vis-à-vis this basket, they will enjoy more stable real effective exchange rates.[34] In particular, they will be less susceptible to dollar-euro and dollar-yen fluctuations. By tracking similar baskets, they can also achieve more intraregional exchange rate stability. Singapore has already been managing its exchange rate in a manner that resembles this G-3 currency basket system.[35] Korea and Thailand, without any formal commitment, appear to have adopted something resembling this system in recent years.[36] It can be argued that China and Malaysia also took first steps in this direction in July 2005.

A G-3 basket would also afford protection against the possibility of a sharp fall in the value of the dollar. If the U.S. twin deficits and East Asian payments surpluses persist, downward pressure on the dollar will eventually intensify. If East Asian currencies have to rise against the dollar, it is desirable that they do so in an orderly fashion. As Masaru Yoshitomi notes in chapter 2, there will be a reluctance to let individual Asian currencies rise against the dollar unless the central banks and governments responsible for their movement have reason to think that their Asian neighbors will also allow their currencies to rise. (In the absence of such reassurance, the initiating countries would fear a double loss of competitiveness in the United States and East Asian markets.) By agreeing on regionwide adoption of a G-3 currency basket, countries will have in place a mechanism through which this response can be coordinated.

China is particularly important in this connection, given its prominence in East Asian trade and investment flows. Thus it would be desirable if the Chinese authorities allowed the renminbi to exhibit greater flexibility so that it could be part of this group of Asian countries that made policy with reference to the G-3 currency basket and so that it could move together with the other East Asian currencies. While Yoshitomi argues that coordinated adjustments could be made on a largely ad hoc basis, I argue here that coordination would be greatly facilitated by the adoption of formal G-3 currency baskets.

These measures to protect the economies of the region against sharp moves in the value of the dollar would also be a stepping-stone toward the creation of a currency zone in East Asia. Such a zone may be characterized by exchange

34. A point also made by Reinhart and Reinhart (2003).

35. Without officially verifying the constituent currencies and basket weights, as noted above.

36 . See Kawai (2002) and the empirical analysis above.

rates that are relatively stable vis-à-vis one another while exhibiting greater flexibility against the dollar. Following the European example, the transition to a more integrated monetary zone could be navigated in three steps. East Asian countries would start by intensifying the coordination of their economic policies, agreeing on a G-3 currency basket, and creating an Asian Currency Unit (ACU) for use in gauging the collective movements of East Asian currencies vis-à-vis external currencies such as the dollar and the euro. They would then intensify policy coordination by establishing an Asian Snake or Asian ERM. This further coordination of policies would eventually set the stage for establishment of an Asian Monetary Union.

The first stage would commence with the adoption of the aforementioned common G-3 currency basket, with Japan maintaining its flexible rate. The exact degree of exchange rate stabilization undertaken in each case would still depend on country-specific conditions and preferences. This would be the point where the participating countries could create a common unit of account—an Asian Currency Unit (ACU)—which includes the thirteen currencies of the ASEAN+3 grouping.[37] Similar to the European Currency Unit (ECU), the weights of the regional currencies would reflect the relative importance of the countries in the region. The ACU could be used to invoice and settle trade-related transactions and serve as the currency of denomination for bond issues. It could be used to measure each currency's deviation from the regional average.[38]

The economies of the region may also wish to strengthen their liquidity provision mechanism (the Chiang Mai Initiative, or CMI), their regional economic surveillance, and their bond market development initiatives. Strengthening the CMI would entail enlarging its credits, multilateralizing currency swap arrangements, and further loosening the linkage with International Monetary Fund (IMF) programs and conditionality. Enlarging the CMI must also be accompanied by enhanced surveillance to address earlier concerns that a liquidity fund that lent too generously with too little conditionality might create moral hazard for governments on the receiving end—as well as for investors with stakes in the countries in question.[39] Ideally surveillance would be strengthened by creating a professional, independent secretariat capable of

37. The ASEAN+3 countries are the members of ASEAN plus China, Japan, and South Korea.

38. For a complementary approach to using an Asian Currency Unit as a path to regional monetary integration, see chapter 7 by Eichengreen.

39. See Kawai (2002, 2005a), Kuroda and Kawai (2002), Bird and Rajan (2002), and Montiel (2004) for reviews of the recent initiatives undertaken by ASEAN+3 finance ministers. Girardin (2004) discusses issues related to information exchange and surveillance, while Rajan and Siregar (2004) propose to establish a centrally administered reserve pooling system.

formulating adjustment policies in the event of a liquidity crisis and, to the extent necessary, encouraging effective private sector involvement.

Once there is real progress in these areas, East Asia will have effectively established a de facto Asian Monetary Fund (AMF) that can contribute to regional financial stability without creating fears of moral hazard. The challenge is thus how to transform the current economic review and policy dialogue process occurring under ASEAN+3 into best practice surveillance like that conducted by the Group of Seven, the European Union (through its Monetary Committee and Economic and Financial Affairs Council, or ECOFIN) and the Organization for Economic Cooperation and Development, or OECD (through its Economic Policy Committee, Economic Development and Review Committee, and Working Party 3).

To accelerate the process of economic integration, the East Asian economies should go beyond bilateral FTAs, such as those between Japan and Korea, Japan and ASEAN, China and ASEAN, and South Korea and ASEAN. They should start contemplating the creation of an East Asia-wide FTA. Regional trade agreements need to avoid a counterproductive "noodle bowl" of bilaterals by ensuring that harmonized rules, standards, and procedures are introduced in the region and by maintaining consistency with the WTO.

As emerging East Asia and Japan become more integrated, achieve greater economic convergence, and establish stronger supporting institutions, they will be better able to commit to meaningful policy coordination. Ultimately this will make possible the development of a common framework for intra-East Asian exchange rate stabilization covering both emerging East Asia and Japan. Technically, this can be achieved either by increasing the yen's weight in the common G-3 currency basket system or by establishing an Asian Snake or an Asian Exchange Rate Mechanism. The first option would represent de facto formation of a yen bloc, while the latter, more symmetric approach would require all economies, including Japan, to cooperate in stabilizing their exchange rates—possibly with each economy pegging its currency to the ACU.[40]

Extensive financial support would be needed to sustain this sort of multilateral system. This would have to be a fully elaborated short-term liquidity

40. An alternative for the emerging East Asian economies might be to bypass the G-3 currency basket system and to directly adopt the ACU-based system, which would ensure intra-East Asian exchange rate stability. A problem with this alternative approach is that it requires an independent nominal anchor for East Asia—either by allowing one dominant country's central bank to take a lead role in monetary policymaking with other central banks following, or by deciding jointly the group's overall monetary policy. Given the difficulty of resolving this problem in the immediate future, it may be more realistic for emerging East Asia to begin with a G-3 currency basket system as a transitional arrangement, before creating more favorable conditions for an intraregional exchange rate stabilization mechanism.

arrangement—in addition to a full-fledged AMF—capable of undertaking frequent interventions in foreign exchange markets. Macroeconomic policy coordination would have to intensify further. In particular, monetary and fiscal policy rules designed to lend credibility to the exchange rate stabilization scheme would be required at this stage.

Subsets of countries among which the degree of economic integration is greatest—Japan and South Korea; or China and Hong Kong; or Singapore, Malaysia, and Brunei—may wish at this stage to initiate more ambitious subregional currency stabilization schemes. Europe's experience has amply illustrated that a subset of countries can intensify monetary and exchange rate policy coordination without precluding the possibility that others can join them later.

The final stage of the transition is the adoption of a common monetary policy and delegation of policymaking authority to a supranational regional authority. This would be tantamount to the introduction of a single regional currency. Moving to this final stage would require a high level of political solidarity and significant political leadership from Japan, China, Korea, and ASEAN.

Conclusion

The creation of the euro is only the first of a series of regional challenges to the global key currency role of the dollar. In East Asia, market-based economic integration is likely to continue, fostering the emergence of an autonomous economic zone comparable in many respects to the European Union. If so, the formation of a tri-polar currency system based on the dollar, the euro, and one or more Asian currencies is a plausible scenario for the future.

The question is under whose initiative and leadership the Asian currency zone may take shape. Will the dominant Asian currency be the Japanese yen, the Chinese renminbi, or a collection of Asian currencies?

The answer will depend in part on how the economic prospects of the issuing countries evolve. The importance of this evolution is evident from past experience. The regional role of the yen diminished in the 1990s, as Japan lost a decade to stagnant economic growth. Even had Japanese economic performance been better, the slow progress of yen internationalization would have made it difficult for Japan to create an Asian currency zone by itself.

As for the international role of the renminbi, decades will have to pass before China completes its transition to a market economy, fully liberalizes its capital account, transforms its financial system, eradicates poverty and income disparities, improves domestic governance, and consolidates political transition. Until that happens, the renminbi will not be used by the residents of other countries as comfortably and extensively as the dollar and the euro. Other East Asian countries like Singapore, however robust their policies and institutions, are too small for their currencies to take on a meaningful international role.

This renders it desirable to pursue exchange rate stabilization and monetary integration in the region by utilizing the yen, the renminbi, the won, the baht, and other East Asian currencies in combination. Agreement on the adoption of a common currency basket—composed of the G-3 currencies of the U.S. dollar, the euro, and ACU—as the reference point for exchange rate and monetary policies would be a first step in this direction. But moving from there to deeper integration involving an enhanced role for Asian currencies other than the yen would also require that governments strengthen the Chiang Mai Initiative and regional surveillance, and establish a regionwide infrastructure for bond markets, while at the same time working to build mutual trust and political consensus.

Given that Japan is still the largest economy in the region, what role should it play? Japan can provide impetus for regional integration, monetary and other wise, by further liberalizing the access of its neighbors to its markets in goods, services, money, capital, labor, and information. It can broaden and deepen its financial markets and move back to higher productivity growth, thereby making international use of the yen more attractive to international investors, if only as part of a basket of major currencies. It can offer leadership in creating an East Asian economic community by encouraging agreement on common rules for trade and investment. Finally, it can provide a monetary anchor for East Asia by pursuing a stable monetary policy, thereby emulating the role played by Germany in Europe.

But Japan cannot go it alone. In the same way that monetary integration in Europe required a commitment by both France and Germany, monetary integration in Asia will require a commitment from both China and Japan. But just as the process was facilitated by the existence in Europe of a currency with deep and liquid markets, the deutsche mark, around which efforts at deeper regional integration could be organized, the process of Asian monetary integration could be greatly eased by continued efforts by Japan—for the internationalization of the yen, the pursuit of stable monetary policies, and more generally a renewed commitment to regional integration. And just as political solidarity in Europe was fostered by leadership by Germany in overcoming the country's historical enmity with France, the political solidarity needed for effective monetary integration in Asia could be fostered by political reconciliation between the two great powers in that region.

References

Bird, Graham, and Ramkishen S. Rajan. 2002. "The Evolving Asian Financial Architecture." *Essays in International Economics* 226. International Finance Section, Department of Economics, Princeton University (February).

Calvo, Guillermo, and Carmen Reinhart. 2002. "Fear of Floating." *Quarterly Journal of Economics* 117: 370–408.

Dooley, Michael, David Folkerts-Landau, and Peter Garber. 2005. *International Financial Stability: Asian Interest Rates and the Dollar.* New York: Deutsche Bank.

Eichengreen, Barry. 2006. "China's Exchange Rate Regime: The Long and Short of It." University of California–Berkeley (March).

Eichengreen, Barry, and Tamim Bayoumi. 1999. "Is Asia an Optimum Currency Area? Can It Become One? Regional, Global and Historical Perspectives on Asian Monetary Relations." In *Exchange Rate Policies in Emerging Asian Countries,* edited by Stefan Collignon, Jean Pisani-Ferry, and Yung Chul Park, pp. 347–66. London: Routledge.

Frankel, Jeffrey A. 2005. "On the Renminbi: The Choice between Adjustment under a Fixed Exchange Rate and Adjustment under a Flexible Rate." Working Paper 11274. Cambridge, Mass.: National Bureau of Economic Research (April).

Frankel, Jeffrey A., and Andrew K. Rose. 1998. "The Endogeneity of the Optimum Currency Area Criterion." *Economic Journal* 108: 1009–25.

Frankel, Jeffrey A., and Shang-jin Wei. 1993. "Trade Blocs and Currency Blocs." Working Paper 1335. Cambridge, Mass.: National Bureau of Economic Research (April).

Friedman, Milton. 1953. "The Case for Flexible Exchange Rates." In *Essays in Positive Economics,* pp. 157–203. University of Chicago Press.

Girardin, Eric. 2004. "Information Exchange, Surveillance Systems and Regional Institutions in East Asia." In *Monetary and Financial Integration in East Asia: The Way Ahead,* edited by the Asian Development Bank, vol. 1, pp. 53–95. Houndmills and London: Palgrave-Macmillan.

Goto, Junichi, and Koichi Hamada. 1994. "Economic Preconditions for Asian Regional Integration." In *Macroeconomic Linkage: Savings, Exchange Rates, and Capital Flows,* edited by Takatoshi Ito and Anne Krueger, pp. 359–85. University of Chicago Press.

Hernandez, Leonardo, and Peter J. Montiel. 2003. "Post-Crisis Exchange Rate Policy in Five Asian Countries: Filling in the 'Hollow Middle'?" *Journal of the Japanese and International Economies* 17: 336–69.

Kawai, Masahiro. 1987. "Optimum Currency Areas." In *The New Palgrave: A Dictionary of Economics,* edited by John Eatwell, Murray Milgate, and Peter Newman, vol. 3, pp. 740–43. London: Macmillan Press, Ltd.

———. 2002. "Exchange Rate Arrangements in East Asia: Lessons from the 1997–98 Currency Crisis." *Bank of Japan Monetary and Economic Studies* 20 (special issue): 167–04.

———. 2005a. "East Asian Economic Regionalism: Progress and Challenges." *Journal of Asian Economics* 16: 29–55.

———. 2005b. "Trade and Investment Integration and Cooperation in East Asia: Empirical Evidence and Issues." In *Asian Economic Cooperation and Integration: Progress, Prospects and Challenges,* edited by the Asian Development Bank, pp. 161–93. Manila: Asian Development Bank.

Kawai, Masahiro, and Taizo Motonishi. 2005a. "Macroeconomic Interdependence in East Asia: Empirical Evidence and Issues." In *Asian Economic Cooperation and Integration: Progress, Prospects and Challenges,* edited by the Asian Development Bank, pp. 213–68. Manila: Asian Development Bank.

———. 2005b. "Is East Asia an Optimum Currency Area?" Revised version of a paper presented to the High-Level Conference on Asia's Economic Cooperation and Integration organized by the Asian Development Bank, Manila, July 1–2.

Krugman, Paul R., and Maurice Obstfeld. 2003. *International Economics: Theory and Policy.* 6th ed. New York: Addison-Wesley.

Kuroda, Haruhiko. 2004. "Transition Steps in the Road to a Single Currency in East Asia." Paper delivered to the Asian Development Bank Seminar, "A Single Currency for East Asia—Lessons from Europe," Jeju Island, South Korea, May 14.

Kuroda, Haruhiko, and Masahiro Kawai. 2002. "Strengthening Regional Financial Cooperation in East Asia." *Pacific Economic Papers* 51, Australian National University.

Kwan, C. H. 2001. *Yen Bloc: Toward Economic Integration in Asia.* Brookings.

McKinnon, Ronald I. 1963. "Optimum Currency Areas." *American Economic Review* 53: 717–25.

———. 2005. *Exchange Rates under the East Asian Dollar Standard.* MIT Press.

Montiel, Peter J. 2004. "An Overview of Monetary and Financial Integration in East Asia." In *Monetary and Financial Integration in East Asia: The Way Ahead,* edited by the Asian Development Bank, vol. 2, pp. 1–2. Houndmills and New York: Palgrave-Macmillan.

Mundell, Robert A. 1961. "A Theory of Optimum Currency Areas." *American Economic Review* 51: 657–65.

Rajan, Ramkishen, and Reza Siregar. 2004. "Centralized Reserve Pooling for the ASEAN+3 Countries." In *Monetary and Financial Integration in East Asia: The Way Ahead,* edited by Asian Development Bank, vol. 2, pp. 285–329. Houndmills and New York: Palgrave-Macmillan.

Reinhart, Carmen, and Vincent Reinhart. 2003. "What Hurts Most? G-3 Exchange Rate or Interest Rate Volatility?" In *Economic and Financial Crises in Emerging Market Economies,* edited by Martin Feldstein, pp. 133–66. University of Chicago Press.

Tavlas, George S. 1993. "The 'New' Theory of Optimum Currency Areas." *World Economy* 16: 663–85.

Wilson, Dominic, and Roopa Purushothaman. 2003. "Dreaming with BRICs: The Path to 2050." Global Economics Paper No. 99. New York: Goldman Sachs (October).

6

GONGPIL CHOI

Toward an Exchange Rate Mechanism for Emerging Asia

THE MERITS OF alternative exchange rate arrangements for emerging Asia continue to be discussed extensively. Proposals range from calls for the establishment of common basket pegs and coordinated floats to blueprints for a single regional currency. The reasons for this interest are not hard to find. Given the extent of intra-Asian trade, the development of intra-Asian supply chains, and the growth of intra-Asian foreign direct investment (FDI), fluctuations in individual Asian currencies can have a significant impact not only on the issuing countries but also on their neighbors. Thus the preoccupation with regional exchange rate arrangements and not just individual country decisions reflects an important reality.

At the same time, the theory of optimum currency areas (OCAs) suggests that countries with different economic characteristics will prefer different exchange rate regimes, creating a challenge for efforts to agree on a common regional arrangement. Large economies like China will understandably prefer relatively flexible exchange rates—or so, at least, the theory suggests—since these allow them to tailor monetary policy to economic conditions that are largely determined at home. In contrast, smaller, more open economies like Hong Kong will prefer to peg their currencies, since they value the simplicity and hence the stimulus to their trade. This creates obvious challenges for any scheme for coordinating exchange rates within the region.

Moreover, even if there is agreement on a desirable degree of exchange rate stability, there remains the question of stability relative to what. For example, now that China has begun moving toward greater exchange rate flexibility, Hong Kong faces the dilemma of whether to manage its exchange rate with reference to the dollar or the renminbi. While this problem is particularly pressing for Hong Kong, the dilemma is general. Increasingly China's large size and rapid rate of growth render its policies too consequential to be ignored. Thus the evolution of China's exchange rate arrangements poses a challenge for the entire region. As the renminbi begins fluctuating more freely against the dollar, there will be an additional reason why other Asian countries may wish to see their currencies fluctuate more freely against the dollar as well. Insofar as America's chronic current account deficit implies that the dollar will have to fall significantly against other currencies, not least against the renminbi, this dilemma becomes more acute. Thus the question is not simply whether China can smoothly navigate the transition to greater exchange rate flexibility vis-à-vis the dollar but also whether other Asian countries can do likewise, and whether the ways in which they adjust their exchange rate regimes will be compatible.

This chapter presents a proposal for finessing this problem through the creation of an Asian Exchange Rate Mechanism, or AERM. Initially, emerging Asian countries participating in the AERM would agree on a common basket of external currencies—the dollar, the euro, and the yen—as a reference point for their policies. But, in recognition of their differing economic characteristics and circumstances, they would not commit to pegging their currencies to this common basket with a common degree of rigidity. Asian countries that valued currency stability vis-à-vis the rest of the world would adopt relatively rigid pegs against this basket, while other Asian countries that preferred more monetary room for maneuver would shadow the common basket at more distance, allowing their currencies to exhibit more flexibility against it. Since some emerging East Asian currencies would fluctuate more than others against the external basket, they would also display some variability vis-à-vis one another.

Over time, as intra-Asian trade and investment continue to expand, the participating countries will come to prefer a greater degree of exchange rate stability vis-à-vis one another. They can achieve this within the framework of the AERM by harmonizing their policies vis-à-vis the common extraregional basket. For example, they could agree to accept more flexibility relative to that common basket; if they all implemented that commitment in the same way, so that their currencies moved against the common external basket more or less in parallel, they would then enjoy more currency stability vis-à-vis one another. Over time, then, greater harmonization of policies would lead the focus of emerging East Asian exchange rate policies to shift from extraregional to intraregional exchange rate stability. In this way, the AERM would allow a glide path—that is, a gradual transition—to a common East Asian exchange rate policy.

Admittedly, the policy harmonization contemplated in this study is no easy task. For it to work, it will be essential to create an institutional counterpart to these exchange rate rules, an "Asian Exchange Rate System" through which the coordination of policies can take place. Thus in addition to describing a basic set of exchange rate arrangements, this chapter sketches the broader institutional framework in which it will be embedded.

The second section starts with some initial considerations designed to draw out what is distinctive about the emerging East Asian case. In particular, it explains why policymakers attach such importance to exchange rate stability. In a world of multiple regions, however, this still begs the question of "stability against what"—against other Asian currencies or the currencies of the rest of the world? This is the focus of the third section. The fourth section then presents a proposal for an exchange rate mechanism for emerging East Asian countries. The fifth section considers the special role of Japan in such a system. The sixth section discusses alternative monetary anchors, such as inflation targeting, as this mechanism evolves away from its initial focus on stability vis-à-vis extraregional currencies. The seventh section concludes and offers some suggestions for further research.

Initial Considerations

Loosening the links between Asian currencies and the dollar would not be an entirely bad thing. If the correction of global imbalances implies a period of slow U.S. economic and import growth, then Asian countries may no longer be able to rely so heavily on the United States as a market for their exports. Tracking the exchange rates of other countries that become increasingly important as destinations for the products of Asian industry will then become correspondingly more important. In addition, the dominant position of the dollar as a vehicle and reserve currency may ultimately be eroded by America's sustained trade and financial imbalances. This is yet another reason why Asian central banks and governments may ultimately prefer to manage their exchange rates with reference to a basket of currencies rather than just the dollar.

Whatever exchange rate regime is chosen by Asian governments and central banks, there will still be the need for an anchor for monetary policy. Simply advising countries to embrace greater exchange rate flexibility is not sufficient guidance for the formulation of monetary policy. Guillermo Calvo has famously observed that floating is not a monetary policy strategy; it is the absence of a strategy (Calvo 2000). Here there exists a range of alternatives. Central banks can target inflation, as Japan has sought to do. Or they can shadow a basket of foreign currencies, as Singapore and a growing number of Asian countries have done with some success. If they opt for the second alternative, they can concentrate on either regional or extraregional currencies.

But these national decisions should not be taken in isolation from one another. National monetary policies can be a significant source of cross-border spillovers, as analyzed in the classic literature on competitive devaluations and in more recent work on crises and contagion. Such spillovers are of particular consequence in regions like Asia where economic and financial interdependencies are extensive. Thus whatever option is chosen as the basis for the central bank's monetary policy operating strategy, it should be taken with the need for a nominal anchor and the consequences for neighboring countries in mind.

Finally, the comparison with Europe, with its long history of currency cooperation, points to two distinctive aspects of the environment for currency cooperation in Asia.[1] First, there is the importance of ensuring that any new regional exchange rate regime is compatible with financial stability. Europe experienced a series of financial disturbances as it navigated the transition to monetary union in the early 1990s.[2] Given Asia's own history of financial crises, policymakers there attach even greater priority to avoiding any repetition of this experience. Thus the choice of regional exchange rate regime needs to be evaluated in terms of its implications for financial stability in addition to the standard criteria such as implications for exports, output, and inflation.

Second, there is the special difficulty of achieving the requisite macroeconomic and financial cooperation in the absence of a commitment to political integration. While the European drive for political integration has its limits (recall French and Dutch voters' rejection of the EU Constitution in their referenda in the summer of 2005), Asian enthusiasm for political integration is, if anything, even more limited. Given the differences between Europe and Asia in political context, the relatively centralized, politically driven approach to monetary integration that culminated in the creation of the euro may not be feasible in the Asian case. In Asia, in contrast to Europe, policymakers and the public many prefer a more market-led, decentralized approach.

In Asia, stable exchange rates have traditionally been regarded as synonymous with robust economic growth. Exchange rate volatility has the undesirable effect of discouraging exports, particularly to the U.S market. It is widely

1. For more on this comparison, see chapter 4 by Shin and Wang.

2. The definitive analysis of this history is Buiter, Corsetti. and Pesenti (1998).

argued that nominal volatility is more damaging to trade than in the advanced industrial countries, given the absence of well-developed forward and futures markets on which risks to profitability can be hedged. It is seen as more corrosive to price stability, given that pass-through from exchange rate swings to inflation is even higher than in the advanced industrial economies.

In addition, for countries where international financial liabilities are heavily dollarized, exchange rate volatility can jeopardize financial stability. In emerging markets with heavily dollarized liabilities, abrupt depreciation can destabilize the financial system by raising the cost of servicing and repaying external debts. This is clearly evident in the behavior of credit ratings and spreads, which are adversely affected by depreciation and devaluation: more so even in countries where external liabilities are denominated in foreign currency than elsewhere.[3] These differences between emerging and advanced industrial economies may explain the well-known reluctance of the former to tolerate large exchange rate movements.[4]

Stable against What?

Even if one accepts these arguments for stable exchange rates, there remains the question of "stable relative to what?" A variety of potential reference points exist for exchange rate policy, not all of which have the same benefits in terms of stability and growth. Asian countries can peg to the dollar, the yen, the euro, a euro-yen-dollar basket, or one another's currencies (in this last case mimicking the operation of Europe's multilateral currency grid). John Williamson argues that since Asian countries export not just to the United States but also to Europe, Japan, and other parts of the world, a basket peg may have superior performance characteristics to an individual currency peg.[5] The stability of the effective exchange rate, which is what matters in this context, can thus be enhanced by stabilization against a basket of currencies. Real effective exchange rates for the major East Asian countries are shown in figure 6-1. (For the kind of evidence that Williamson cites, see table 6-1.)

But while a common basket peg may be appealing in principle, there are difficulties implementing it in practice. As is often the case in exchange rate economics, the proof of the pudding is in the eating. For one thing, different

3. Evidence on this appears in Eichengreen, Hausmann, and Panizza (2003).

4. This is emphasized in the literature on "fear of floating" (see for example Calvo and Reinhart 2002).

5. See for example Williamson (2005).

Figure 6-1. *Real Effective Exchange Rate Movements of Selected Asian Countries, before and after the 1997 Crisis, 1990–2005*[a]

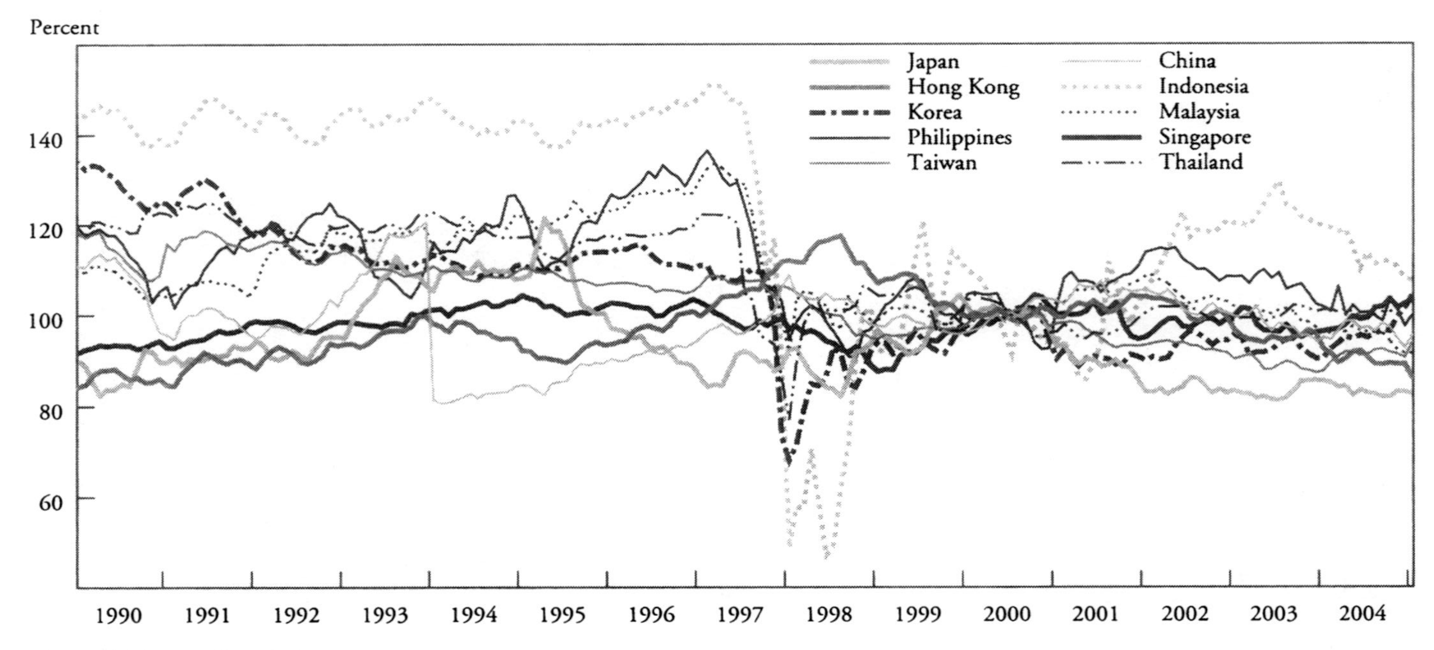

Source: JP Morgan Chase database.

a. Data are monthly averages. Higher values indicate appreciation of the domestic currency.

Table 6-1. *Standard Deviations of East Asian Currencies and Baskets, 2000–04*[a]
Percent

Country	*Historical experience*	*Individual country peg*	*Common basket peg*
China	5.78	2.62	1.54
Hong Kong	4.50	4.67	1.54
Indonesia[b]	2.23	2.68	1.54
Malaysia	4.04	3.74	1.54
Philippines	6.53	3.72	1.54
Singapore	2.56	3.52	1.54
South Korea[c]	2.90	4.04	1.54
Taiwan[b]	4.41	4.10	1.54
Thailand[c]	2.59	3.33	1.54

Source: Williamson (2005).

a. Standard deviations of period-end monthly nominal effective exchange rate; January 1995 = 100.

b. Data for Indonesia and Taiwan (end-month) are from Thomson Datastream Series JPMIDNB (Indonesia) and NTDTWER (Taiwan).

c. Data for South Korea and Thailand (end-month) real effective exchange rates are from the Citibank CTERI Database.

baskets are appropriate for different objectives. If the goal is to encourage intra-Asian trade, then a country may wish to peg to a basket of Asian currencies. But insofar as the goal is to encourage trade with the rest of the world, then it may be desirable to peg to a basket of extraregional currencies. Thus two options are available: one in which each Asian country uses a basket that includes other regional currencies, and one in which it uses a common basket of extraregional currencies.

The two objectives can be pursued simultaneously, of course, if each Asian country pegs to the *same* set of extraregional currencies. This observation has prompted calls for emerging East Asian countries to agree on a common basket peg.[6] Again, however, doing so is no easy task. Some countries may be concerned with export growth and wish to maximize stability vis-à-vis their principal trading partners. Others may be more worried about financial stability and seek to maintain stability vis-à-vis the country or countries from which they borrow and the currencies in which their external liabilities are denominated. And even if they can agree on the priority to be attached to

6. Thus Ito, Ogawa, and Sasaki (1998) and Williamson (1999) have argued that East Asian governments should respond by agreeing on a system of collective basket pegs with weights on the dollar, yen, and euro.

trade and financial considerations, the identity of their principal export markets and most important sources of external finance will differ. So too, therefore, will appropriate basket weights.

Then there is the question of how rigidly to maintain the peg. If the authorities adopt very wide bands or engage in frequent realignments to prevent the buildup of speculative pressures, their commitment to stabilize the exchange rate will be vested with relatively little credibility. There will be no "bias in the band"—no tendency for the exchange rate to move less, relative to fundamentals, as the edges of the fluctuation band are approached.[7] As a result, the resulting regime will differ little from floating in practice. On the other hand, if countries adopt very narrow bands and operate their pegs rigidly, they expose themselves to speculative pressures, may experience financial instability, and will have little scope for tailoring monetary conditions to local needs (defined as either national and regional needs). Since the credibility of policy and the shadow price of flexibility will differ across countries, so too will preferences regarding the optimal point on the trade-off between stability and flexibility. As with the weighting scheme for the common basket peg, there will be no single point on that trade-off that will, in general, be optimal for each one of a heterogeneous group of countries. For all these reasons, collective action on exchange rate issues is not easy.

Against this backdrop, agreement on a plan of action would be facilitated by the creation of an institutional mechanism for resolving conflicts of sovereign interest: that is, by creating a venue where information can be shared and consensus can be reached about the desirable properties of a common basket peg and about the extent to which it is necessary to adjust national policies to account for the effects of cross-border spillovers within the region. The fifth section describes how such a venue should be designed. But first, the next section presents a specific proposal for a multilateral exchange rate arrangement for emerging East Asia: an Asian Exchange Rate Mechanism, or AERM.

Designing the Asian Exchange Rate Mechanism

The proposed AERM has two components. First, Asian countries would agree on a common reference basket of foreign currencies. Second, they would take individual national decisions about how strictly to track that basket—about how rigidly to peg—consonant with differences in their economic character-

7. The term in quotation marks originates with Krugman (1991).

istics. Thus while in all cases the reference point for monetary policy would be the same, each country would still have leeway to decide how closely to track the common external basket.

To be sure, this second set of decisions would have important cross-border implications: the decisions of individual countries would have implications for their neighbors. In particular, their decisions would determine how strictly Asian currencies are stabilized against one another. Thus it is desirable that those decisions be taken in mutual consultation. But this does not mean that they must be identical.

This approach is not without precedent. In the first decade of the European Monetary System (EMS), while the majority of countries participating in the EMS maintained their exchange rates within 2.25 percent bands, Italy and several new entrants were initially permitted to maintain wider bands (6 percent).[8] Countries were similarly allowed to realign by different amounts and with different frequency, so long as those decisions were taken in mutual consultation. This history suggests that the existence of a variety of national arrangements can be compatible with the operation of a regional system, so long as decisions regarding the rules of the game are taken collectively. The history of the EMS also serves as a reminder of the dangers of attempting to place all participating countries in the same monetary straitjacket. It is a reminder of the risks of attempting to operate narrow bands, given high capital mobility, and of pursuing a monetary policy strategy that places excessive emphasis on defending those bands. Singapore has had more success, in part, as a result of deemphasizing its band and stressing the importance of monetary stability and credibility. The EMS crises of 1992–93 caution against the alternative.

At the conclusion of these consultations, some participating countries would presumably opt to peg rigidly to the common external basket, while others might prefer a significantly greater degree of flexibility against it. As a result, their bilateral rates would continue to fluctuate. Exchange rate variability would be a fact of financial life. This situation would not be comfortable, but emerging East Asian countries cannot have it both ways—they cannot have both exchange rate stability vis-à-vis the dollar and exchange rate stability vis-à-vis the renminbi when the dollar and the renminbi have a growing tendency to fluctuate against each other.[9] If the reference currencies have a tendency to fluctuate, then individual Asian countries would have to decide to which ones they prefer to peg and against which ones they would be willing to float.

8. For details, see De Grauwe (2005).

9. One can substitute "yen" for "renminbi" and "Asia" for "emerging Asia," and the point would remain the same.

This observation, together with the presumption that emerging East Asian countries will continue to attach importance to exchange rate stability vis-à-vis the dollar and the euro for some time to come, has uncomfortable implications for Asian monetary and financial integration. A substantial literature has documented the benefits of exchange rate stability for financial development and integration. Asian governments have made cooperation in the development of national financial markets a priority, as manifested in the establishment of the Asian Bond Fund and the Asian Bond Market Initiative. Continued variability of exchange rates within East Asia will discourage cross-border participation in local markets by Asian investors, other things equal, and slow the growth of local currency bond issuance. Such variability is also likely to slow the growth of the intra-Asian trade that East Asian governments seek to cultivate as an alternative to excessive dependence on the U.S. market. These are all reasons why a situation of continuing intraregional currency flexibility will not be an entirely happy one.

One way of squaring this circle would be through the creation of an Asian currency unit as a parallel Asian currency, as proposed by Barry Eichengreen in chapter 7 of this volume. This synthetic unit would be a composite—a weighted average—of the underlying Asian currencies and enjoy full legal tender status in the participating countries. As a weighted average of national currencies, it would be more stable in terms of aggregate intraregional trade and payments than any one constituent currency and thus might emerge over time as an attractive unit in which to invoice and settle intraregional transactions and in which to issue Asian bonds. As the parallel currency gains market share, Asia would effectively be readying itself for the eventual adoption of a single currency.

In the early stages of this process, it would not be necessary to stabilize the exchange rates between the constituent national currencies; these could continue to fluctuate against one another. Countries would thus be free to continue pegging to an extraregional basket if they so wished (they could chose extraregional exchange rate stability over intraregional exchange rate stability). But at the same time there would exist a stable regional currency unit whose properties were conducive to the expansion of intraregional trade and financial transactions and whose presence promoted cross-border participation in local financial markets.[10]

10. As noted by Williamson (2005), this parallel currency approach is compatible with the adoption of a common external basket peg in the early stages of development of the AERM. In other words, there is no incompatibility between creating a synthetic unit that is a weighted average of East Asian currencies and at the same time pegging those East Asian currencies, individually or as a group, to a common external basket.

With the growth of intra-Asian trade and investment, emerging East Asian countries would presumably come to prefer a higher level of intraregional exchange rate stability. They would be able to achieve this within the same framework if they harmonized their decisions about how closely to track the common external basket. This will be equally true whether they all agree to adopt rigid pegs relative to the common external basket or whether they all decide to float against the common external basket in parallel and to the same extent. To reiterate, saying that the participating countries should agree to harmonize their policies toward the common external basket is not the same as saying that they should increase the stability of their currencies against the common external basket. To the contrary, they could agree instead that it would be desirable for all the participating Asian countries to see their currencies exhibit more flexibility against the common extraregional basket. But if they harmonized their policies and their individual currencies all fluctuated against the common external basket in similar fashion, they would then fluctuate less vis-à-vis one another.

Thus whatever the exchange rate rule followed by the participating countries, the adoption of a common rule and harmonization of the associated policies would ensure that their currencies had an increasing tendency to move together.

Agreeing on a common basket peg, modifying its weights periodically, and accounting for the cross-border implications of national policy decisions would entail extensive consultation. In the later phases of the operation of the AERM, the close harmonization of national policies would require even more regular and intensive discussions.

This is an argument for creating a standing committee of policymakers of the participating countries, whose members would meet together on a regular basis: say, monthly. In many countries, decisions regarding the exchange rate regime are vested with the government rather than the central bank; thus the relevant discussions should involve finance ministers as well as central bank governors. National treasuries and central banks could provide input into their deliberations.

A more ambitious option, whose implementation would presumably become easier at a later date, would be to create a permanent secretariat for the AERM, charged with monitoring policies as well as providing input into policymakers' deliberations. Most ambitious of all would be to make that secretariat autonomous by funding it with financial contributions from the participating countries and giving its director and senior staff security of employment (and thus insulation from political pressure). While an autonomous secretariat empowered to exercise "firm surveillance" in the true sense of the phrase would be a departure from the Asian way of not overtly criticizing one's neighbors, creating an entity with these powers would be essential to ensure the adequate coordination of national policies.

These institutional arrangements might be seen as a stalking horse for an Asian central bank, in the same sense that the EMS was a stalking horse for EMU. More generally, the creation of these permanent transnational institutions and the transition toward closer policy harmonization within the region could thus be seen as first steps in the direction of creating a common Asian currency.

As the participating countries seek to stabilize their currencies more strictly vis-à-vis one another, financial supports will become more important. Currency stabilization agreements create targets at which foreign exchange speculators can shoot, and mutual financial assistance will be needed to ensure that regional central banks and governments have the ammunition necessary for mounting a defense. The ASEAN+3 countries have in place some $40 billion of bilateral swaps and credits under the umbrella of the Chiang Mai Initiative (CMI). The CMI could be used as the foundation for the requisite financial supports, assuming that disbursal was made automatic and no longer contingent on negotiation of an International Monetary Fund (IMF) program—something else that would be feasible only in the presence of strong mutual surveillance.

The Role of Japan

An important question in this connection is whether Japan would participate in the AERM or whether the arrangement would be constituted as an exchange rate mechanism for *emerging* East Asian economies. Would the yen be part of the common external basket to which emerging East Asian countries pegged in the first phase, or would it instead be one of the participating Asian currencies that was managed in harmonized fashion and that therefore fluctuated in tandem against the common external basket in the second?

Japan is sufficiently important to emerging East Asian countries as a source of export demand and foreign direct investment that they presumably would be reluctant to exclude the yen from the common basket that they shadowed at the outset of their arrangement. But if Asian countries moved over time toward replacing stability vis-à-vis the external basket with stability among the currencies of the participating countries, then a common basket that included the yen, against which other Asian currencies now floated with increasing freedom, would be unattractive. Thus there is no easy solution to this dilemma.

Removing the yen from the common external basket at a later stage and allowing Japan to then join the AERM would solve this problem, but changing the composition of the common external basket in midstream would be an additional complication that would make the operation of the system and the establishment of credibility more difficult in practice.

Is Inflation Targeting an Alternative?

The alternative to currency pegs as an anchor for monetary policy is inflation targeting. Inflation targeting is challenging in emerging markets for three reasons.[11]

—Emerging markets are relatively open. Forecasting inflation is especially difficult in open economies, since different exchange rate–related channels linking the central bank's instruments and targets operate with very different lags.

—In emerging market economies, financial liabilities are often denominated in foreign currencies, as noted above. As a result of the difficulty they have in borrowing abroad in their own currencies, financial institutions and their customers will have currency mismatches on their balance sheets. Under these circumstances, an inflation targeting central bank will be reluctant to let the exchange rate move: it will be unable to benefit from the greater flexibility ostensibly offered by that regime. These observations suggest that inflation targeting will be less attractive, the more open the economy.[12]

—The less robust is the policy credibility of the central bank, the less attractive inflation targeting will be. In practice, policymakers in emerging markets often lack credibility. In such countries, the history of central bank independence is relatively brief. Political pressure to pursue a range of alternative policy objectives is intense. There thus may be fears that the monetary authorities will be responsive to those pressures and less than fully committed to the pursuit of low and stable inflation. Thus the only way for the central bank to credibly signal its commitment to price stability may be for it to peg to the currency of a country known for its commitment to this target.

In practice, these three distinctive features of the environment in which monetary policy is conducted in emerging markets have implications for one another. For instance, in countries where the adverse balance sheet effects of liability dollarization dominate only when exchange rate movements reach a certain point, conventional inflation targeting may still be viable so long as

11. As explained at greater length in Choi (2003), from where the discussion in this section is drawn.

12. Note the consonance of this argument with a key implication of the theory of optimum currency areas.

shocks and corresponding exchange rate movements are relatively small.[13] Such countries will wish to target inflation flexibly by adjusting monetary policy in response to large exchange rate movements, while regarding small movements with benign neglect. Unfortunately, even limited amounts of flexibility can be destabilizing when credibility is lacking. A central bank that temporarily disregards a surge in inflation in order to, say, stabilize the financial system may find its commitment to price stability questioned. Credibility problems will force precisely those emerging markets where a flexible approach to inflation targeting is most valuable to adopt a relatively rigid version.

What then is the role of inflation targeting in the Asian Exchange Rate Mechanism envisaged here? The answer depends on whether the participating countries move over time to more or less flexibility relative to the common external basket. A variety of arguments—some of which were already mentioned in the introduction to this chapter—suggest that they will in fact come to prefer greater flexibility against extraregional currencies like the dollar and the euro. If so, with the external exchange rate anchor cut adrift, they will then need an alternative anchor for monetary policy. East Asia does not obviously possess a currency anchor equivalent to the deutsche mark in the European Monetary System.[14] Here inflation targeting is a viable substitute. It is not a perfect solution to the problem, since its implementation in emerging markets is not straightforward. But it is still better than the available alternatives (including monetary targeting and nominal GNP targeting). By agreeing on a common level or common upper and lower thresholds for target inflation, Asian countries can acquire the monetary anchor they require as they allow their currencies to fluctuate more freely against the dollar and the euro while limiting their variability vis-à-vis one another.

Conclusion

The Asian Exchange Rate Mechanism proposed in this chapter would follow the precedent of Europe in the 1980s and 1990s by creating a framework within which cooperative decisions on regional exchange rate policy could be reached. But Asian countries differ from their European counterparts in the high value they attach to exchange rate stability vis-à-vis extraregional curren-

13. On this, see Eichengreen (2000).

14. Arguably, only Japan and China are large enough to serve in the anchor role. But the Bank of Japan has not exactly been a paragon of price stability in recent years, while China maintains capital controls and uses a variety of nonmarket instruments in the conduct of monetary policy, which hardly makes its currency an attractive anchor for the monetary policies of other countries in the region.

cies, as opposed to stability vis-à-vis one another's currencies. Thus where European countries created a multilateral currency grid designed to stabilize their currencies against one another, emerging East Asian countries need—and for the foreseeable future will continue to need—a rather different arrangement to stabilize their exchange rates vis-à-vis their extraregional trading partners including the United States, Europe, and Japan (taking the latter as outside *emerging* East Asia).

To be sure, the countries of emerging East Asia value intraregional currency stability as well, since this is important for promoting intraregional trade, encouraging cross-border participation in local currency bond markets, and setting the stage for the eventual creation of a single Asian currency. They will surely come to attach even greater value to intraregional exchange rate stability over time, as the volume of intra-Asian trade and financial flows continues to expand. Moreover, squaring this circle will become more difficult as the major Asian currencies, notably the Chinese renminbi, exhibit greater flexibility against the dollar. Asian countries will thus face the dilemma of having to choose between two objectives.

The Asian Exchange Rate Mechanism sketched in this chapter provides a partial solution to this problem. Initially, emerging East Asian countries would agree on a common basket of G-3 currencies to provide a reference point for their national monetary policies. They would take individual national decisions about how closely to track it, as a result of which their currencies would continue to fluctuate against one another. Over time, as intra-Asian trade and investment expands relative to extra-Asian trade and investment, they would come to attach higher priority to intraregional exchange rate stability relative to extraregional exchange rate stability. By then harmonizing their policies toward the common external basket, they would be able to enhance the stability of intraregional exchange rates. If they harmonize how they track the common dollar-euro-yen basket, in other words, they would succeed in stabilizing their currencies vis-à-vis one another. If that decision involves following the dollar, euro, and yen at a greater distance, priority would have been shifted from extraregional to intraregional exchange rate stability.

Saying that Asian countries should harmonize their policies is easy, but actually doing so is hard. Harmonization would require firm surveillance to verify that governments are adhering to their commitments, and the creation of a venue for frank discussions to ensure that the common thrust of policies is broadly acceptable to all participating countries. Strengthening East Asian surveillance processes and policy dialogues is a necessary first step in this evolution. But it would have to be followed by significant additional institution building for the Asian Exchange Rate Mechanism envisaged here to become a reality.

References

Buiter, Willem, Giancarlo Corsetti, and Paulo Pesenti. 1998. *Financial Markets and European Monetary Cooperation.* Cambridge University Press.

Calvo, Guillermo A. 2000. "Capital Markets and the Exchange Rate, with Special Reference to the Dollarization Debate in Latin America." University of Maryland at College Park.

Calvo, Guillermo A., and Carmen M. Reinhart. 2002. "Fear of Floating." *Quarterly Journal of Economics* 117: 379–408.

Choi, Gongpil. 2003. "Structural Changes and the Scope of Inflation Targeting in Korea." *International Economic Journal* 17: 113–142.

De Grauwe, Paul. 2005. *The Economics of Monetary Union.* Oxford University Press.

Eichengreen, Barry. 2000. "Can Emerging Markets Float? Should They Inflation Target?" University of California–Berkeley.

Eichengreen, Barry, Ricardo Hausmann, and Ugo Panizza. 2003. "Currency Mismatches, Debt Intolerance and Original Sin: Why They Are Not the Same and Why It Matters." Working Paper 10036. Cambridge, Mass.: National Bureau of Economic Research. (October).

Ito, Takatoshi, Eiji Ogawa, and Yuri Sasaki. 1998. "How Did the Dollar Peg Fail in Asia?" NBER Working Paper 6729. Cambridge, Mass.: National Bureau of Economic Research. (September).

Krugman, Paul. 1991. "Target Zones and Exchange Rate Dynamics." *Quarterly Journal of Economics* 106: 669–82.

Williamson, John. 1999. "The Case for a Common Basket Peg for East Asian Currencies." In *Exchange Rate Policies in Emerging Asian Countries,* edited by Stefan Collignon, Jean Pisani-Ferry, and Yung Chul Park, pp. 327–44. London: Routledge.

———. 2005. "A Currency Basket for East Asia, Not Just China." Policy Briefs in International Economics PB05–1. Washington: Institute for International Economics.

7 BARRY EICHENGREEN

Parallel Processes? Monetary Integration in Europe and Asia

PARALLELS ARE FREQUENTLY drawn between monetary integration in Europe and monetary integration in Asia, both by those who argue that Asia should emulate Europe's example and by others warning that it should not. Like Europe in the 1950s and 1960s, Asia has achieved a remarkable expansion of intraregional trade, strengthening the argument for a cooperative arrangement to prevent trade flows from being disrupted by exchange rate fluctuations. As in Europe, the growth of foreign direct investment (FDI) and regional supply chain linkages has heightened the sensitivity of producers and investors to exchange rate–related problems. And, not unlike Europe's experience with the breakdown of the Bretton Woods system in the 1970s, the Asian crisis of 1997–98 and now fears of an impending dollar crash have created a desire for a cooperative monetary process to prevent exchange rates and financial conditions from being disturbed by extraregional factors.

At the same time, Asia's experience is seen as a warning of the dangers of proceeding with monetary integration in advance of political integration and of the fragility of a common basket peg in a world of high capital mobility. The 1992 crisis of the narrow-band European Monetary System (EMS), which came hot on the heels of the removal of capital controls, is a reminder of the first danger.

This chapter draws on a study undertaken by the author for the Asian Development Bank on the parallel currency approach to Asian monetary integration. None of the opinions expressed here are necessarily those of that organization or any other with which the author is affiliated.

This episode also revealed that strong currency countries were willing to take only limited steps to support their weak currency partners in a world of sovereign states and independent central banks. The advent of the euro might be thought to have eliminated these fragilities, but by creating an accountability deficit, because of the absence of an institutional counterweight to demand political accountability of the European Central Bank (ECB), it only fanned tensions among European Union (EU) member states and between governments and their citizens. These came to a head with French and Dutch rejection of the EU constitution in the spring of 2005, precipitating talk of the reintroduction of national currencies. To the extent that the prospects for political integration are even more limited in Asia, the implication is that pursuing the European route of a common basket peg leading ultimately to a regional currency is more problematic still.

But there is also another example from Europe that might be emulated to more positive effect: the parallel currency approach to monetary integration.[1] Rather than replacing national currencies with a single Asian currency, participating governments could instead create a parallel currency (the Asian Currency Unit, or ACU for short), constituted as an appropriately weighted average of Asian currencies, and allow it to circulate alongside their existing currencies. Importers and exporters worried about the risk of quoting prices or being obligated to settle their transactions in a national currency other than their own, whose value can fluctuate, may find it attractive to denominate those transactions in a parallel currency that allows them to diversify away those risks. Issuers of foreign debt may find it more attractive to denominate their securities in the parallel currency rather than in dollars or a single Asian currency other than their own, while foreign investors may find it attractive to add such securities to their portfolios. With the progress of economic and financial integration, the advantages of using the parallel currency as a unit of account, means of payment, and store of value will become increasingly pronounced. The ease of transacting in the parallel currency will provide further stimulus to intraregional trade and investment. It will provide a unit convenient for transacting on bond markets and pursuing other cross-border activities to whose growth and development currency risk is an obstacle. And as those markets and activities continue to develop at the regional level, the attractions of transacting in the parallel currency will in turn become increasingly evident.

A parallel currency can also provide a glide path—that is, a smooth transition—to monetary union. When a suitably high fraction of transactions is

1. Thus the double entendre in the title of this chapter is intentional.

conducted using the parallel currency, it will be clear that Asian countries are economically prepared for monetary union. National currencies can then be converted into the parallel currency at prevailing exchange rates, and monetary unification will be a fait accompli. This last step will of course require political will as well as economic preparation; specifically, it will require the willingness to create a regional central bank along the lines of the ECB that answers to no single national government. But, under the parallel currency approach, it will be clear that Asia is economically ready for the transition when that last political step is finally taken.[2]

The disadvantage of the parallel currency approach is the risks it poses for financial stability. From the perspective of each participating country, the ACU is an amalgam of foreign currencies.[3] As banks, firms, households, and governments use the parallel currency in a growing range of transactions, they will acquire positions and exposures in those foreign currencies. This can be a source of balance sheet mismatches that give rise to financial fragility. Countries can limit these risks by applying the conventional prudential measures, such as capital controls and regulations limiting currency mismatches in the financial sector. But controls and regulations that limit the use of the parallel currency will also slow the transition to monetary union.

Thus while the parallel currency approach has attractions as a route to monetary union, it is likely to be a slow one. For those who read European history as a reminder of the dangers of a premature move to monetary union, this is not a bad thing. For others who regard it as imperative that Asia move in this direction sooner rather than later, the parallel currency approach will consequently lack appeal.

The Parallel Currency Approach in Europe

The first mention of the parallel currency approach to my knowledge was in a report in 1972 by the Federal Trust.[4] This proposed redenominating existing eurodollar claims in a parallel currency, the Europa. The authors of this document were concerned with a different problem—the eurodollar overhang—

2. I am not the first to develop this idea. Mori, Kinukawa, Nukaya, and Hashimoto (2002) have proposed the creation of an Asian Currency Unit as a way of creating an environment in which the private sector can participate in the discussion of monetary integration and contribute to its development. Aggarwala (2003) has proposed the creation of a parallel currency as an initial step toward a single currency for South Asia.

3. And of the home currency as well, which also has a weight in the underlying basket.

4. See Magnifico and Williamson (1972).

but their report helped put the parallel currency idea on the table. The idea was then taken up in the "All Saints' Day Manifesto" published in the *Economist* magazine on November 1, 1975.[5] In 1990 the U.K. government presented a draft treaty embodying these ideas as a contribution to the debate over the Delors Report.[6] A type of parallel currency, the European Currency Unit (or ECU), had a formal role in the operation of the European Monetary System from the outset of the latter in 1979. Subsequent years saw the development of a market in financial assets denominated in ECUs: not just official claims issued and held by central banks and governments but also private ECUs issued and held by nongovernmental entities.

In the end, however, the road running through the parallel currency led nowhere. Understanding why requires a digression into the history of the ECU. The ECU was first defined in 1974 as a basket of specified amounts of the currencies of the members of the European Community for purposes of EC accounting. It was adopted in 1975 as the unit of account for the European Development Fund. It was later adopted as the unit of account for the European Investment Bank and for the budget of the Community, since the Community would have found it difficult to denominate its budget in the currency of any one member country, given the tendency for exchange rates to fluctuate.

The next step was the establishment of the European Monetary System and its Exchange Rate Mechanism (ERM) in March 1979. Because intra-European exchange rates were held reasonably stable through the operation of the ERM, the ECU was in turn reasonably stable against the constituent currencies—a fact that was supposed to be part of its appeal.[7] In principle, all countries participating in the ERM were supposed to stabilize their exchange rates against the ECU basket. Currency positions acquired as the result of interventions were to be settled using the ECU or, alternatively, the creditor's currency or the dollar.

In practice, however, the additional role for the ECU was limited. Although credits within the ERM were denominated in ECUs, they were actually extended in national currencies. Rather than actually basing ERM parities on an ECU central rate, the central rate was only used to compute bilateral rates, which became the focus for market attention and central bank policy.

5. "All Saints Day Manifesto," *Economist* (November 1, 1975), pp. 33–38.

6. See U.K. Treasury (1990).

7. While the United Kingdom and Greece did not participate in the ERM from its outset, their currencies were included as components of the ECU (the drachma from 1984, when Greece joined the Community).

Official ECUs were created by the European Monetary Cooperation Fund in exchange for three-month swaps of 20 percent of the gold and dollar reserves of EMS central banks. Through this process official ECUs were added to the reserve portfolios of the participating central banks. Central banks were authorized to use official ECUs to repay their borrowings from other central banks, subject to various restrictions. The official ECU was not convertible for transactions with entities other than the participating central banks. It maintained its value equal to the underlying basket of national currencies only because the central banks that undertook transactions in ECUs agreed to value it that way. In effect, the official ECU was simply a different name for a portion of European central banks' gold and dollar reserves.

If the ECU was to gain currency (as it were), this would have to be because importers, exporters, and financial market participants took it up. In practice a small but active market in private claims denominated in ECUs developed quickly. A private ECU was a claim by one private entity on another: for example, a claim by a depositor on a private financial institution issuing an ECU-denominated bank deposit, or the claim of a bondholder on a private corporation issuing an ECU-denominated bond. Private ECUs could thus be purchased with and redeemed for the components of the basket. The value of the private ECU was guaranteed by the commitment of the issuer (such as the commitment of the private bank issuing the deposit) to convert the derivative instrument into its underlying components at par. Until the fall of 1988, a group of major European banks that made the market in this instrument stood ready to buy and sell private ECUs at the official price. In effect they acted like a currency board, buying and selling private ECUs as needed to keep their price fixed.[8]

Commercial banks then began dealing in ECUs in order to be able to handle these official deposits. In turn this facilitated the growth of private ECU deposits. Some banks saw this as a promising line of business: they invested in the development of a bilateral clearing system in ECU deposits out of which eventually developed a multilateral clearing system. By the middle of the 1980s, the ECU had become the fourth largest non-dollar currency in

8. At that point, however, they grew concerned about the extent of their exposures and discontinued the practice of fixing the rate. From that point the price of the private ECU varied relative to the value of its official counterpart. There were limits on the extent of permissible variation as a result of arbitrage: if the price of a non–interest-bearing ECU claim exceeded the cost of purchasing the underlying constituent currencies, investors would have an incentive to sell that claim and buy those currencies—and have profits left over. But the effectiveness of arbitrage was limited by transaction costs, which could be substantial when what was involved was not just selling one asset for another, but selling one composite asset and buying ten currencies, the markets in some of which were relatively illiquid.

Eurocurrency markets, following the deutsche mark, the Swiss franc, and the yen. The majority of ECU bank claims were interbank deposits. With the spread of ECU-denominated claims, the ECU came to be widely traded on the interbank market outside Europe as well as in the region. More than 20 banks in the United States traded ECUs as of the mid-1980s. An active interbank market in ECUs also developed in Hong Kong and Singapore. This suggests that if a parallel Asian currency takes off, it will also be traded outside the region.

The other segment of the private ECU market was bonds.[9] The growth of the ECU bond market will be a comforting observation for Asian policymakers for whom promoting the development of regional bond markets is a priority. By the mid-1980s ECU bonds accounted for about 18 percent of all non-dollar Eurobonds. The ECU was the third largest currency of issuance for non-dollar Eurobonds behind only the deutsche mark and sterling. ECU medium-term notes appeared at the beginning of 1988, and by the early 1990s they accounted for about 16 percent of the non-U.S. dollar market in such notes. By the beginning of the 1990s, there was also a considerable market in ECU commercial paper, amounting to about 10 percent of all Eurocommercial paper.

Thus the ECU quickly took on at least some of the characteristics of a parallel currency. It was used as a unit of account, store of value, and means of settlement by the institutions of the European Community. It was accepted in settlement to a limited extent outside the borders of the Community. It was quoted on foreign exchange markets. Forward as well as spot markets soon developed. Writing in 1986, Allen concluded that the ECU was beginning to function as a full-fledged parallel currency.[10]

Notwithstanding these positive signs, authors like Paul De Grauwe characterize European experience with the ECU as a failure.[11] The ECU was never widely used as a medium of exchange; the bulk of transactions in Europe continued to be conducted in national currencies, not just European currencies but also dollars.[12] Its unit of account role was essentially limited to the institutions of the European Community and a very few European corporations engaged in

9. In addition, other securitized claims such as forwards, futures, currency swaps, options, and syndicated credits denominated in ECUs were also offered by the ECU bank markets and exchanges. Durrant (1991) describes the growth and operation of these markets.

10. See Allen (1986).

11. See for example De Grauwe (1992).

12. In Italy, where the instrument was most extensively used for settling international transactions, only about one half of 1 percent of imports and exports were settled in ECUs as of the mid-1980s (Allen 1986). By 1989 the share of the ECU in the invoicing of exports and imports was 0.5 and 2.4 percent, respectively (Fujita 1995).

extensive cross-border business. An obvious unit of account role would have been in international trade, but as late as the 1990s only about 1 percent of trade within the Community was denominated in ECUs.[13] Another obvious use would have been as a unit in which to denominate international bonds; despite some growth here, at the end of 1989 only 4 percent of the outstanding stock of bonds issued in international markets was denominated in ECUs.

Measures of market turnover are lacking, but contemporary commentary notes that the markets in bank assets were relatively illiquid. Deposits generally did not extend beyond one year, in contrast to deposits in the major currencies, which were available for terms as long as five years. Markets for ECU-denominated bank acceptances and commercial paper were even less liquid and less well developed. Markets for ECU-denominated derivative instruments (futures, swaps, options) were shallower and less liquid still. Richard Levich argues that the explanation for the illiquidity of these derivative markets was the failure of the ECU to assume the basic functions of a currency on a significant scale.[14] He argues that if agents do not do everyday business in ECUs, they will have little incentive to use the associated derivative markets to hedge risks in ECUs.[15]

The question then is why the ECU was not used more widely as a currency. The immediate explanation lies in the maintenance of capital controls through the 1980s in many European countries. Typically, the same limits that were placed on the freedom of residents to transact in foreign currencies also applied to the ECU. Europe was not ready in the 1980s for free and open capital markets, nor had its exchange rate system been adapted to the realities of such an environment. In this setting, controls were still essential, and they limited the spread of the ECU as a parallel currency.

More fundamentally, the failure the ECU to be used more widely points up the limitations of any basket-based regional unit as a parallel currency. The basket definition of the ECU may be attractive to investors, especially investors from small countries for whom claims denominated in domestic currency provide limited diversification. But a basket-based unit has few intrinsic advantages as a medium of exchange or unit of account, especially so long as the largest share of day-to-day transactions continues to take place within national borders, and domestic wages and prices are denominated in the national currency.

13. See Jozzo (1989).

14. See Levich (1987).

15. As he puts it, "If the ECU fails to perform the services of money, then it seems unlikely that any ECU-denominated product, no matter how cleverly engineered is likely to find a market niche. The 'moneyness' of the ECU is the key factor" (Levich, 1987, p. 10).

In addition, coordination problems may prevent market participants from individually utilizing the parallel currency as a medium of exchange even if they have a collective interest in doing so. As the European Community grew progressively more integrated, it was conceivable that Europe's residents would have been better off conducting the bulk of their transactions in ECUs rather than some of them conducting them in francs, others in marks, others in lira, and so forth. But there existed changeover costs deterring any one resident from unilaterally moving in this direction in the absence of the knowledge that others were doing the same. It was unattractive for individual European producers to quote prices in ECUs unless other European producers did so, limiting transaction costs. It was unattractive for individual financial institutions to float bonds denominated in ECUs unless other financial institutions did the same, creating the critical mass needed for a deep and liquid secondary market. It was unattractive to quote product prices in ECUs so long as wages and other domestically sourced inputs were priced in the national currency.

Money is characterized by network externalities; it pays to use the same medium of exchange and unit of account as other market participants (Dowd and Greenaway 1993). As with any network, there may be a tendency for the status quo to be locked in. Governments can attempt to make the parallel currency more attractive by giving it full legal tender status alongside the national currency, permitting its use for, among other things, tax payments. But this perspective from the theory of network externalities suggests that the incentive to continue relying on the national currency will remain strong even if this is the case. As a means of payment for day-to-day transactions, adoption of the parallel currency may have to overcome considerable historical inertia; the decision of whether to shift to another currency has the nature of a coordination game, in which no one agent has an incentive to move unless he is confident that the others with which he does business will move as well. Thus absent a major shock that renders the use of national currencies less attractive—and experience suggests that the shock in question would have to be very large to prompt significant currency substitution—or a policy initiative such as announcing a decision to make the parallel currency the sole legal tender at some firm future date, there is reason to doubt that use of the parallel currency will quickly crowd out the use of national currencies.[16]

The other source of inertia was of course the international role of the U.S. dollar (another parallel, as it were, with obvious relevance to Asia). A substan-

16. Klein (1978), in an early comment on the parallel currency proposal, can be seen as anticipating this problem.

tial fraction of European countries' commercial and financial transactions with other European countries and the rest of the world were invoiced and settled in dollars. This international vehicle currency provided many of the same advantages—low currency conversion costs, transparency in pricing—as a parallel European currency. In addition it had the advantage of incumbency; it was already widely used. As a currency in which to denominate financial instruments, the dollar continued to dominate not just the ECU but also sterling and the deutsche mark in the Eurobond market all through the 1980s. In the Asian context, where the U.S. dollar is also used for many international transactions, one can similarly question whether an ACU can successfully outcompete it.

This is not to imply that the ECU market would have forever remained a quiet backwater or that the parallel currency was doomed to fail as a mechanism for monetary integration. But it is a reminder that pursuing the parallel currency route to this destination is bound to take time. For those who see monetary integration as welfare improving only when it is driven by economics rather than politics, this is not necessarily a bad thing.

Mechanics

As noted, the ECU developed in conjunction with the European Monetary System and its Exchange Rate Mechanism, a multilateral grid of currency pegs. Central rates were officially defined in terms of ECUs, although currencies were de facto pegged to the value of the other participating countries. Establishment of the ACU could similarly be the occasion for participating countries to agree on a set of common basket pegs corresponding to the composition of the ACU basket.[17] But it would also be possible to establish the ACU as a parallel currency defined as a basket of the currencies of the participating countries without adopting a common basket peg—and, for that matter, without any peg at all, aside from a set of rules and interventions that maintains the ACU's value relative to the specified basket of regional currencies. If the constituent currencies float against one another, then the ACU will rise in value relative to currencies that depreciate against the basket and fall in value relative to currencies that appreciate against the basket, without its value changing relative to the basket as a whole. Thus there is a logical distinction between the decision to establish a parallel currency defined as a basket of regional currencies and the decision to adopt a harmonized system of currency pegs.

17. For more on this, see the sixth section.

The advantage of marrying the two steps is that the parallel currency will be stable against all of the constituent currencies, not just their average—a fact that should encourage its use. More precisely, it will be stable against all the constituent currencies, assuming that the regional pegging arrangement continues to hold. This restatement also points to the disadvantage of pegged rates: namely, their fragility in a world of high capital mobility. Making agreement on a common basket peg a prerequisite for issuing the parallel currency and for initiating the transition to monetary union would expose the participating countries to a significant risk of currency crises. Indeed, it can be argued that the advantage of the parallel-currency approach is precisely that agents can begin to adapt themselves to the fact of a regional currency without requiring exchange rates between national currencies first to be locked, something that would dangerously heighten crisis risk and potentially derail the monetary unification process.

The All Saints' Day Manifesto suggested that national central banks should issue the parallel currency against national currencies: in other words, that the parallel currency would be fully backed by and convertible into national monies. Once sufficient confidence in the new currency developed, the Manifesto continued, central banks could be allowed to rediscount bills, make loans to the banking system, and use open market operations to inject additional supplies of the parallel currency into circulation. At this point backing in national currencies would be less than 100 percent, but confidence would presumably be strong enough to support the practice.

Aggarwala's proposal for a parallel Asian currency, in contrast, suggests that the new currency would be issued against a pool of foreign exchange reserves, presumably dollars and euros, not a pool of national currencies. Central banks would transfer, say, 10 percent of their foreign reserves to an "Asian Monetary Fund" or "Asian Reserve Fund." (The term "Asian Monetary Fund" has a history and is politically loaded; the discussion that follows therefore refers instead to an "Asian Reserve Fund," or ARF.) In addition, in Aggarwala's proposal, issuance of the parallel currency would be a multiple of the reserves of the ARF from the start. That portion not backed by foreign exchange reserves would be backed by and issued in conjunction with purchases of national government bonds.

The idea that the ARF should hold dollars and euros as reserves echoes the currency board model appropriate for an entity seeking to keep its currency stable against an extraregional currency. In the current case, Asian central banks would contribute dollar reserves (or some combination of dollar and euro reserves), with the goal of keeping the ACU stable against the dollar (or against some combination of the dollar and the euro). But creating a common

Asian currency whose value is fixed relative to the dollar (or relative to some combination of the dollar and the euro) is not obviously the goal of the current enterprise. Rather, the goal here is to create a regional unit that preserves its value and is stable against a basket of Asian currencies. In this case it would be more appropriate for the participating central banks to contribute their own currencies, as suggested by the All Saints' Day Manifesto. If the ACU showed signs of depreciating against one or more regional currencies, the Asian Reserve Fund would then purchase ACUs, selling the relevant regional currencies out of its reserve.

It would still be possible to keep the price of the parallel currency fixed to a basket of the currencies of the countries participating in the arrangement despite the absence of 100 percent currency backing. This is simply a pegged exchange rate, in contrast to a fully backed currency board. However, a partially backed system, as a de facto pegged exchange rate, could be vulnerable to speculative attack. The liabilities of the Asian Reserve Fund, as the equivalent of a composite of national currencies, would exceed the value of the national currencies in its possession. It would have issued additional ACUs, above and beyond those backed by the national currencies contributed by the participating central banks, by purchasing bonds, discounting commercial paper, and the like, presumably in the participating countries (and presumably denominated in their currencies). In the event of a run on its reserves precipitated by a shock that led to a decline in the value of those assets, the ARF might not be able to buy up sufficient quantities of ACUs to prevent its price from falling, absent credit lines and swaps from the national central banks, which might or might not be forthcoming in sufficient amounts.

Thus there is likely to be a trade-off between full backing in regional currencies of issuance of the parallel currency, which would maximize confidence, and the size of the initial issuance, on which secondary market development and liquidity are likely to depend.

As noted above, there are reasons to doubt that simply agreeing on the definition of the ACU as a basket of Asian currencies and giving the new unit legal tender status in the participating countries would suffice to prompt the growth of a significant market. While a basket may have superior risk/return characteristics to an individual currency, it is not obvious that an Asian basket would have superior performance characteristics to any number of other baskets that might be assembled by financial market participants. A derivative security indexed to a basket of currencies may be less costly to purchase than the components of the underlying basket, but it will be attractive to hold and trade only in the presence of liquid secondary markets. Without an installed base of ACU bonds, the initial securities issued in this unit would be relatively illiquid; there would not be much of a secondary market on which they could trade.

Thus if the liabilities of the Asian Reserve Fund are to be fully backed by a share of regional foreign exchange reserves, there may then be an argument for Asian governments and transnationals to issue ACU-denominated bonds, maintain ACU deposits, and settle their accounts among themselves in ACUs in order to create a larger installed base of ACU securities and jump-start the secondary market. National governments and the Asian Development Bank (ADB) could fund themselves by issuing ACU bonds. Initially, doing so might require these issuers to compensate purchasers of their bonds for the relative illiquidity of the ACU market, but this could be regarded as a small price to pay for opening the way to a feasible transition to monetary union.

In principle it would be possible to allow clearing of these transactions in ACUs through cooperating banks. This is how the clearing of private ECU claims began in Europe in 1983, when a group of banks opened ECU accounts with one another, agreed to act as correspondent banks for other banks dealing in ECUs, and netted and cleared ECU claims multilaterally among themselves. This arrangement was expanded with the establishment of the ECU Banking Association in 1985, whose members were made responsible for managing the ECU clearing system and working toward its improvement. Transactions between member banks took place across accounts held by the participating banks at the Bank for International Settlements (BIS). SWIFT provided the transmission mechanism for payments messages and computed balances for each bank vis-à-vis the others. One could imagine a similar arrangement in Asia, with clearing across accounts at the BIS, which conveniently maintains a Hong Kong office.

That the BIS is not primarily an Asian institution has encouraged talk of an Asian clearing system. There have been a number of concrete proposals for an Asian Clearing System, or "Asia Clear." The first was probably the suggestion of the former treasurer of the Asian Development Bank in 1992. This idea failed to take off because of rivalry about where the new facility should be located and because there was not yet enough business to support such a system.[18] Bilateral links between the national clearing facilities and central securities repositories of different countries were pursued instead, under the leadership of the Hong Kong Monetary Authority. In 1998 the Asia-Pacific Central Depository Group of eighteen national central securities depositories (NCSDs) conducted a feasi-

18. Mori, Kinukawa, Nukaya, and Hashimoto (2002) have suggested establishing a centralized facility for ACU transactions in Singapore or Hong Kong. They suggest that an organization like the Central Moneymarkets Unit of the Hong Kong Monetary Authority might be utilized for this purpose. However, this idea has not been taken up either, presumably for similar reasons.

bility study of the issue. This led to proposals for linking the clearing and settlement systems of Asian countries through the Internet, avoiding conflict over where to locate the facility. However, bilateral settlement is more costly than centralized settlement, since in the first case each NCSD must maintain an account with each other NCSD. Moreover, the start-up costs of a network of national depositories would be high to the extent that national settlement platforms are not standardized. Seven Asian countries, including Australia and New Zealand, use real time gross settlement and delivery-versus-payment systems, whereas the others do not. This has resulted in the development of relatively few bilateral linkages among Asian NCSDs and disappointing trading volumes.

Alternatively, might ACU-denominated financial claims be settled and deposited through existing international central securities depositories (ICSDs) such as Euroclear and Clearstream? A number of Asian countries, such as Hong Kong, Japan, the Philippines, Singapore, and Thailand, are already linked to Euroclear. Euroclear offers investors a choice of currencies of settlement, including Asian currencies. Insofar as the market for ACU bonds would be international, this would create an obvious market niche for existing ICSDs.

But those ICSDs would presumably offer settlement in ACU only once the market in ACU securities took off. Absent intervention—a payment to Euroclear or Clearstream to induce them to offer settlement in ACUs, or steps to link Asian central banks and NCSDs and a commitment on their part to offer settlement in ACUs—there would be a chicken-and-egg problem. ACU trading would not take off without ACU settlement, but ACU settlement would not be offered without ACU trading. Faced with the choice between a subsidy for Euroclear or an investment in linking regional NCSDs, Asian governments might well be more favorably inclined toward the latter.

Must policymakers think about "convergence criteria" for candidates for inclusion in the parallel-currency basket? It is not obvious that there should be structural or macroeconomic preconditions, similar per capita incomes, or similar business cycles, given that there will still be scope for independent national monetary policies until the parallel currency dominates national currencies in domestic as well as international transactions. It is not clear that there need to be similar inflation rates across participating countries, since national currencies can still fluctuate against one another.

The most difficult question is probably whether the removal of capital controls should be a precondition for inclusion. On the one hand, European experience shows that there is no reason why a parallel currency cannot be created by a group of countries still retaining significant capital controls, since this is what Europe did in the 1980s. For those interested in encouraging the participation of a majority of Asian countries, this is an attractive feature. On the other hand, controls that restrict the access of residents to foreign currencies—and foreign currency composites—will slow the rate of take-up of the parallel currency. Not unlike other strategies for monetary unification, wide participation, and the participation of countries with capital controls in particular, will tend to slow progress toward the ultimate goal.

All this implicitly points to the question of China's participation. China accounts for roughly one third of the East Asian economy. Excluding it on the grounds that it maintains capital controls would make the parallel currency and any future regional currency less attractive, since these would then have no use in the largest economy in the region. On the other hand, including China despite its maintenance of controls would slow the transition to a common regional currency, following the logic laid out above. But pressuring China to remove its controls in order to participate in the project could place financial stability at risk. Of these options, the most sustainable would appear to be the second, which implies relatively slow growth of usage of the parallel currency and a slow transition to monetary union.

Dangers

The downside of the parallel currency approach is the danger it may pose for financial stability. By definition, promotion of a parallel currency is designed to encourage banks, firms, and households to take on ACU-denominated claims. If they end up with mismatches between the value of their ACU liabilities and assets, they will then be subject to heightened financial fragility. If banks match their ACU liabilities and ACU loans (or make more ACU loans than they take ACU deposits), the currency risk will then simply be transferred to their corporate customers (those who take out the loans), saddling the banking system with heightened credit risk. Liquidity risk can also result if depositors are aware of these vulnerabilities and run on the banking system even when more fundamental problems are absent.

The question is whether these risks can be contained by appropriate adjustments of prudential and macroeconomic policies. At a minimum, the preceding observations suggest that prudential supervision and regulation should be tightened to ensure that banks hold enough liquid ACU assets (or constituent foreign currency assets). These same considerations suggest that the central bank and government should hold additional foreign reserves in ACUs or the constituent foreign currencies to enable them to replenish the ACU reserves of the banking system. They suggest that the authorities should move to a managed float to encourage banks and firms to hedge their ACU exposures.

But forcing central banks and governments to hold additional foreign currency reserves may have significant opportunity costs. Encouraging them to limit their net liabilities in ACUs will prevent them from issuing ACU-denominated bonds as a way of creating a benchmark asset and enhancing the liquidity of secondary markets. Forcing the banking system to hold additional foreign currency reserves abroad can limit the growth of intermediation. Moreover, given the gap between the promulgation and enforcement of prudential regulations, it is not even clear that tighter supervision will succeed in containing the risk to stability. The conclusion of much of the literature is that partially dollarized economies should urgently move forward to full dollarization or back toward a predominantly domestic currency basis by installing a sound and stable monetary policy.[19] This suggests than an extended period when the parallel currency circulates alongside national currencies could be one of heightened financial fragility.

The appropriate response to this problem is to strengthen supervision and regulation and corporate governance to ensure that entities incurring ACU liabilities manage these exposures prudently. In particular, this may involve limiting the freedom of banks to accept ACU deposits in excess of their ability to make ACU loans and otherwise restraining the growth of financial markets and transactions in ACU-denominated claims. The problem is that this will further slow growth of the use of the parallel currency. Thus safely navigating the parallel currency route might be an even lengthier process than otherwise supposed.

In Europe there was also considerable worry that establishing a parallel currency would threaten price stability. As commercial banks created claims in the parallel currency, there would be more money and credit chasing the same goods and services. Europe's inflationary problems would then be aggravated, and the economy might experience boom-and-bust cycles that threatened not just price stability but economic and financial stability as well.

Subsequent scholarship has refined the way we think about these issues. Allowing commercial banks to create additional liquidity by accepting additional deposits and making additional loans in ACUs clearly would provide further stimulus to demand and inflation. But ACU transactions would be no different from the other foreign currency transactions of the banking system in this regard. Banks in Asian countries can access foreign funding subject to the

19. This is the conclusion, for example, of De Nicolo, Honohan, and Ize (2003).

standard prudential regulations. They can make foreign currency–denominated loans subject to those same regulatory provisions. There is no intrinsic difference between a Thai bank's accepting dollar deposits and making dollar loans and its accepting ACU deposits and making ACU loans. The solution is for the central bank to use its reserve-management instruments to limit the growth of bank assets and liabilities. In the presence of sound central banking and prudential supervision, in other words, it is not clear that developing the parallel currency should be a threat to price stability.[20]

Would it make a difference if the parallel currency were also used as a means of exchange: for example, as a result of the decision to make it legal tender for domestic transactions, including tax payments? While this would widen the scope for currency substitution, again it is not clear that it would change the situation fundamentally. It would put Asian countries in the same situation as highly dollarized countries in Latin America—economies where the dollar effectively functions as a parallel currency, serving as a unit of account, store of value, and medium of exchange for many transactions.

The Parallel Currency and Proposals for a Common Basket Peg

There are at least two motivations for monetary cooperation in Asia. One is to limit exchange rate variability within the region in order to promote intraregional trade and investment; a parallel currency that gained significant market share would clearly have this effect. The other motivation, manifest in calls for a common basket peg to, inter alia, the dollar, the euro, and the yen, is to buttress exchange rate stability vis-à-vis the rest of the world. Would the parallel currency approach be compatible with this objective as well?

John Williamson notes that there is no incompatibility between the two objectives in principle.[21] There is nothing to preclude a group of countries that adopt a basket of outside currencies as their peg from also creating a basket of their own currencies as a way of establishing a parallel Asian currency, or vice versa. But not only is the rationale for the two strategies different, so too would be the effects. Pegging Asian currencies to the dollar or the euro (or to a basket of which they constitute part) would presumably have the effect of heightening the attractions of these outside currencies for transactions within Asia. Allowing them to float against the euro and the dollar, in contrast, would

20. Of course, strict prudential supervision that limits the capacity of banks to issue ACU liabilities and make ACU investments may slow the development of the parallel currency, as emphasized above.

21. This is discussed in Williamson (2005).

make it more attractive to transact in a unit that was stable in terms of the regional composite as a matter of definition.

Can the ACU Out-Compete the Dollar?

To come into widespread use, the ACU not only must out-compete existing Asian currencies but also must dominate the dollar. Countries such as South Korea and Japan invoice a considerable fraction of their trade in dollars. Such observations have led authors like Robert Mundell to advocate adoption of the dollar as a "common parallel currency"—that is, an official currency to be used for invoicing and settling trade—throughout the Asia region.[22] This problem has obvious parallels in the literature on regional financial development where the question is, similarly, whether developing regional financial markets is a superior alternative to linking into global financial markets that already exist.[23]

There are four arguments on the other side. First, as intra-Asian trade grows relative to trade with the United States, as will presumably be the case as Asian countries continue converging to U.S. income levels and as a result of the further progress of regional integration, invoicing and settling in a common Asian currency will become more attractive relative to invoicing and settling in dollars. Second, Asian countries are reluctant to give the currency of an outside power legal tender status for domestic transactions. As a result, when moving from international to domestic transactions it is still necessary to convert dollars into, say, Thai baht. Under the parallel currency approach, Asian governments would give the ACU full legal tender status; they would also authorize it for domestic use, in other words, which would make it more attractive. Third, there are reasons to think that the dollar will grow more volatile relative to Asian currencies, both as the latter relax and abandon their traditional pegs to the greenback in the interest of greater flexibility and also to the extent that America's chronic twin deficits lead to a weaker dollar; this will make using ACUs rather than dollars more attractive. Fourth and finally, the hold of network externalities and therefore the advantages of incumbency may be less in our financially sophisticated age than in the past. Given the proliferation of instruments in financial markets and the decline in bid-ask spreads, it is easier for market participants to contemplate alternatives.

22. This language is from Mundell (2002).
23. McCauley and Park (2004).

Conclusion

This chapter considered the creation of a parallel currency as an alternative approach to monetary unification in Asia. Its appeal is that the pace would be dictated by economics rather than politics. The take-up of the new currency by the markets would largely dictate the timing of the transition. This is consistent with the greater emphasis placed by the Asian economies on market-led rather than politically led growth since the crisis of 1997–98. It accommodates the fact that the political context is different than in Europe, where the transition to monetary union was driven by an underlying commitment—by no means unquestioned—to political integration. In Asia the commitment to political solidarity and integration is less. This renders it questionable that a politically led process can quickly and smoothly culminate in monetary union. Under the approach sketched here, in contrast, the speed with which private markets adapted themselves to and adopted the new currency would determine the timing of events.

There is still much that officials can do to pave the way for the parallel currency. Constructing a true free trade area and facilitating the further expansion of trade and supply chain networks in the region can make it attractive for the private sector to transact using the parallel currency. By issuing debt denominated in the parallel currency, governments can help create a benchmark asset and more liquid secondary markets, encouraging participation and further issuance by banks and firms. They can make markets in the parallel currency more attractive by investing in the establishment of an efficient regional clearing and settlement system.

To be sure, questions can be raised about how quickly the parallel-currency approach will lead to monetary unification. Even if regional integration renders the parallel currency more attractive as a unit of account, store of value, and medium of exchange, history suggests that it will not be quick to outcompete established national currencies. But if this means that the process culminating in Asian monetary unification will take a considerable number of years to unfold, this need not be viewed as a problem—especially by those who maintain that some years will have to pass before Asia is ready for monetary union.

The main downside of the parallel-currency approach is the risk of financial instability. Allowing banks and corporations to accumulate liabilities denominated in what is in effect a basket of foreign currencies raises the specter of currency mismatches and balance sheet fragility if the initiative is not accompanied by strong market discipline and supervisory oversight of the financial affairs of banks and corporations. It has been observed in other contexts that Asian monetary unification makes little sense unless regional financial systems are first strengthened so that these can accommodate the absence of a unique national monetary policy and a distinct national lender of last resort. In a sense, it is a strength of the parallel currency approach that it makes evident the need for reforms to strengthen supervision and regulation and to enhance investor discipline from the start and not simply at the moment when the national monetary policy and domestic lender of last resort disappear. The analogous weakness is that the transition to a single regional currency might then take even longer than otherwise.

References

Aggarwala, Ramgopal. 2003. "Road to a Single Currency for South Asia." *RIS Policy Brief* 9 (December): 1–4. Research and Information System for Developing Countries.

Allen, Polly Reynolds. 1986. "The ECU: Birth of a New Currency." Occasional Paper 20. New York: Group of Thirty.

De Grauwe, Paul. 1992. *The Economics of Monetary Integration.* Oxford University Press.

De Nicolo,Gianni, Patrick Honohan, and Alain Ize. 2003. "Dollarization of the Banking System: Good or Bad?" Working Paper 03/146. Washington: International Monetary Fund (July).

Dowd, Kevin, and David Greenaway. 1993. "Currency Competition, Network Externalities and Switching Costs: Towards an Alternative View of Optimum Currency Areas." *Economic Journal* 103: 1180–89.

Durrant, Jim. 1991. "The ECU Swaps and Options Market." In *ECU: The Currency of Europe,* edited by Christopher Johnson, pp. 70–84. London: Euromoney Books.

Fujita, Seichi. 1995. "The ECU as an 'Artificial Currency'." *Kobe University Economic Review* 41: 15–29.

Jozzo, Alfonso. 1989. "The Use of the ECU as an Invoicing Currency." In *The ECU and European Monetary Integration,* edited by Paul De Grauwe and Theo Peeters, pp. 148–90. London: Macmillan.

Klein, Benjamin. 1978. "Competing Monies, European Monetary Union and the Dollar." In *One Money for Europe,* edited by Michele Fratianni and Theo Peeters, pp. 69–105. New York: Praeger.

Levich, Richard M. 1987. "Developing the ECU Markets: Perspectives on Financial Innovation." Working Paper 2276. Cambridge, Mass.: National Bureau of Economic Research (June).

Magnifico, Giovanni, and John Williamson. 1972. *European Monetary Integration.* London: Federal Trust.

McCauley, Robert, and Yung-Chul Park. 2004. "Developing Bond Markets in East Asia: Global, Regional or National." Hong Kong and Seoul: Bank for International Settlements and Korea University.

Mori, Junichi, Maoyoshi Kinukawa, Hideki Nukaya, and Masashi Hashimoto. 2002. "Integration of East Asian Economies and a Step by Step Approach towards a Currency Basket Regime." Research Report 2. IIMA (November).

Mundell, Robert. 2002. "Does Asia Need a Common Currency?" *Pacific Economic Review* 7 (February): 3–12.

U.K. Treasury. 1990. "The Hard ECU Proposal." London.

Williamson, John. 2005. "A Currency Basket for East Asia, Not Just China." Policy Briefs in International Economics PB05-1. Washington: Institute for International Economics.

Contributors

Gongpil Choi
Korean Institute of Finance
Federal Reserve Bank of San Francisco

Duck-Koo Chung
Korean National Assembly

Barry Eichengreen
University of California–Berkeley

Masahiro Kawai
University of Tokyo
Office of Regional Integration, Asian Development Bank

Kwanho Shin
Korea University, Seoul

Yunjong Wang
SK Research Institute

Masaru Yoshitomi
Research Institute of Economy, Trade and Industry, Tokyo

Yongding Yu
Chinese Academy of Social Sciences, Beijing

Index

CPSIA information can be obtained
at www.ICGtesting.com
Printed in the USA
LVOW11s0403281017
554120LV00001B/19/P